D1578456

90710 000 483 744

FRANCIS BENALI

FRANCIS BENALI

THE AUTOBIOGRAPHY
Football Man to Iron Fran

WITH MATT BARLOW
FOREWORD BY MATT LE TISSIER

BLOOMSBURY SPORT
LONDON • OXFORD • NEW YORK • NEW DELHI • SYDNEY

BLOOMSBURY SPORT
Bloomsbury Publishing Plc
50 Bedford Square, London, WC1B 3DP, UK
29 Earlsfort Terrace, Dublin 2, Ireland

BLOOMSBURY, BLOOMSBURY SPORT and the Diana logo are trademarks
of Bloomsbury Publishing Plc

First published in Great Britain 2021

A catalogue record for this book is available from the British Library

Library of Congress Cataloguing-in-Publication data has been applied for

ISBN: HB: 978-1-4729-8679-5; eBook: 978-1-4729-8680-1;
ePDF: 978-1-4729-8683-2

2 4 6 8 10 9 7 5 3 1

Typeset in Adobe Garamond Pro by Deanta Global Publishing Services, Chennai, India
Printed and bound in Great Britain by CPI Group (UK) Ltd., Croydon, CR0 4YY

MIX
Paper from
responsible sources
FSC® C020471

To find out more about our authors and books visit www.bloomsbury.com
and sign up for our newsletters

For Karrie, who made all my dreams come true and is always there beside me, and for Luke and Kenz, of everything I have ever done in my life it is you that I am most proud of.
Love you always
Team Benali Forever xx

CONTENTS

FOREWORD
BY MATT LE TISSIER

It was late summer 2014 and I was running with Franny along the canal towpaths adjacent to the M4 motorway. He had decided he was going to run to each of the 20 Premier League stadiums in what was the first of his three challenges. This worked out at about 40 miles a day, every day for three weeks. The scale of it doesn't really hit you until you are there with him, pounding the streets. I joined him for one of the earlier stages and ran for a day. I went home to rest and it took me about two weeks to recover! By the time I joined him again he had covered another 500 miles.

We were on a stretch from Reading into West London, just the two of us, and scheduled to meet the rest of the team for a drinks stop a few miles further down the path when Franny started to say he was struggling with his knee. For him to admit anything like this meant it was serious. Then he slowed down. Then he stopped, and was whacking his knee around with his hand as though the joint had locked and he was trying to free it.

I tried to help, saying, 'Look Franny, it's half a mile until we meet the others, the physio will be there, jump on my back and I'll carry you down the last bit.' He refused, saying, 'No I'll be fine'. I wasn't surprised but tried to reason with him, saying, 'Well, you're not fine mate, you've had to stop running and now you're whacking your knee around, you're obviously not quite right, so just jump on my back.' And that's when he said, 'I'm doing this run and I'm doing it every single step of the way and I'm not going to accept any help from anyone.'

A few minutes later, we were off again, running at quite a slow pace so I could keep up with him. Then we reached the pit stop and he had a bit of physio. Twenty minutes later and he was flying along, back in his rhythm. It would have been easy for him to hop on my back and take the easy route for half a mile. There was nobody around. It was just Franny and me, and I certainly wasn't going to go and tell anyone. Nobody would have ever known the difference but in his mind it was cheating and that was something he would not entertain. He had set himself a challenge and he was going to run every step of the way. That is exactly what he did. Just amazing, that's Franny.

I always knew what he was capable of achieving – I witnessed him in preseason training for all those years. I knew exactly how fit he was and what a machine he was when it came to pushing his body to the absolute limit. He was always the one out at the front on an 8-mile run, coming in 10 minutes before me. He pushed himself. He had the right physique and the right mentality to do it. So I wasn't entirely surprised when he started taking these challenges on. If it was physically possible, I knew Franny had the willpower to do it because his mental strength is something else.

The first time we met, we were schoolboys and I was over in Southampton from Guernsey for training camps in the half-term holidays. I came on trial, quite amazed to find this lad with a fully-grown moustache claiming to be the same age as me. If it was part of his intimidation tactics, it certainly worked. He was a strong and uncompromising centre-forward in those days. He had lots of pace, power and he was banging in a few goals, which might surprise a few people given what came later.

We became good mates down the years, spending a lot of time together, especially in the first year as apprentices when nine of us lived in each other's pockets, making life-long friendships as we tried to forge our careers as footballers.

The way Franny went about it, his desire, professionalism and the way he lived his life were years ahead of his time. When you look at modern players, they do all the right things. But Franny was doing the right things 25 years ago. He realised it was what he needed to have a good career as a footballer. He was the ultimate professional. In terms of dedication and preparation for training and for matches, I did not play with a single player who had a better attitude or approach to his job than Franny Benali.

There were times, obviously, when his passion and determination not to lose boiled over into a few red cards and that was one of the most difficult things for me in our relationship. I knew when the red mist was descending. I knew the signs, the look in his eyes, and I would try to do something about it. There were times when I would be right in his face during the game, trying to calm him down but it was impossible. He would be staring right through me. I could tell he wasn't listening and my efforts were in vain.

The next tackle would be the one that was a fraction late and resulted in a red card. I tried to stop it and I couldn't do it. He became a completely different person when he stepped onto a football pitch. That was the ultra-competitive side of his nature and it was all the more bizarre because at any other time he was the nicest man you could wish to meet. It was as if he had a split personality, like the Incredible Hulk.

It didn't just happen in games, there were times when it happened in training. He would even go for me and I've been one of his closest friends for years. It was an attitude that shaped a terrific career. He was a fighter and if we were in a relegation battle – and at Southampton we were in quite a few over the years – he was the first person I wanted to see alongside me. I knew he would be giving his heart and soul for the next 90 minutes to ensure we did not lose.

That's the way Franny was. He wanted to give his all and do his best, even at times to the detriment of the standard of his play. Sometimes he was so desperate to do well that his natural game did not come through. That might be one thing he could have done a little bit better. He needed to dial it back to find a better balance in his game.

If he could have done that, maybe he would have scored more than one goal but the day he did find the net – after all those appearances and all those occasions with the crowd urging him to shoot when he came within 30 yards of the goal – was the most amazing moment. The only time I can compare the noise level was when I scored the last goal at The Dell. It was the same level of hysteria from the Saints fans.

For me to be the one who lobbed the free-kick onto his head to score made it all the more special. I was so chuffed for him. I was probably more excited to be setting him up for that goal than I was to score 99 per cent of my own goals. To this day, nobody actually knows if he was trying to head it back across goal or going for the goal. He will always say he meant it and as I've been a mate of his for such a long time I totally believe him.

We became much closer over the later years of our careers. As apprentices and young pros, you are so busy scrapping away and trying to get into the first team that you are in your own little world most of the time. We grew closer as we matured. Franny was never a drinker – he was anti-alcohol. I drank Malibu and nobody ever got drunk on that. When everyone was out on the razz, we often weren't and so we had that in common. We were more family orientated. We still share a lot of the same values in life and, of course, we share our love for Southampton Football Club.

Since we've retired as players our friendship has become even closer, which might seem odd considering the amount of time we used to spend together at the training ground, in hotels and travelling on coaches. We are closer than we have ever been and it has been great to see from close quarters exactly what he has achieved with his crazy endurance challenges and charity fundraising in his post-playing career. He has changed all those perceptions people had of him, because if you only ever knew him as Franny Benali the footballer, who had a load of red cards and was a bit too aggressive, then this statement about his true nature will come as a surprise: Franny is probably the kindest and most gentle footballer I have ever come across in my life. I would say that to people when he was still playing and they would all look at me as if I was some kind of a lunatic. I could tell they were thinking, 'Well he can't be, I've seen him on the pitch!'

That is a different Franny Benali. That is Franny Benali the competitor. That is not Franny Benali the husband and father, and friend. People really can have different personalities to those the public see on football pitches.

Matt Le Tissier, Southampton player 1986–2002

PREFACE
TO THE LIMIT

I'm awake in my makeshift bed when I know I should be sleeping. My body is aching and my heart is pounding so fast it feels like it might be about to burst clean out of my chest. My mind is racing.

This doesn't feel right at all. I was troubled by a similar sensation the night before although I kept that to myself because I figured it would be fine in the morning. And it did feel better after some sleep but the day was rough.

The swim was just about bearable but the bike ride was a massive grind. I can't recall ever lifting my head once from the wheel in front of me. The marathon stage was even harder. My vision was blurred and that really did feel weird.

No, I am not in a good place, physically or mentally. I am shattered, completely exhausted.

Serious doubts are forming that I might be unable to complete the challenge I set for myself. To be honest, I am worried about the damage I might be doing to my body. I am worried about my heart. I'm no expert but I'm sure it shouldn't be beating like this when I'm at rest. I ask my wife Karen to put her hand on my chest.

It is the end of Day Four of the 'Iron Fran' endurance challenge, my attempt to complete seven Iron Man triathlons in seven days across the country, finishing in Southampton, the city where I was born and raised, the city I represented for 20 years as a footballer, 16 of them as a professional.

I made 389 appearances for the Saints, the only team I ever wanted to play for, and I was lucky enough to become club captain. We were never relegated from the top flight of English football in all those years, although there were some near misses and narrow escapes. In a sense, we were one of the great underdog stories. At the start of every season we would be tipped to go down and we never did.

We even enjoyed a few successes along the way. In my final season, I was able to play a role as we made it to an FA Cup final, rekindling distant memories of 1976 when our family and friends crowded around the television set to watch Bobby Stokes score the goal to win the Cup for Southampton against Manchester United.

That was me hooked on Saints. I followed Lawrie McMenemy's side as they were promoted to the old Division One, reaching Wembley again in a League Cup final, qualifying to play in Europe, and finishing as runners-up behind Liverpool in 1984.

They signed England stars such as Kevin Keegan and Peter Shilton and were renowned for playing with flair and adventure, and for developing talent in their own youth academy. Matt Le Tissier was the finest player I ever played with (and became my best pal), and Alan Shearer would go on to win the title, captain England and set the record for the most goals scored in the Premier League.

We played for many years at The Dell, a unique and fabulously crooked little ground, where our supporters packed in tightly around the pitch and made life uncomfortable for our opponents.

We had a fearless spirit and competitive courage, which was where I came in handy as the non-scoring full-back. That is not entirely true, because I scored one Premier League goal, a flying header against Leicester, but it is fair to say my reputation was for stopping others, for my aggression, for the ferocity of my tackling and for the red cards.

In total, I was sent off 11 times in Saints colours. That is not a good disciplinary record, but I do like to think supporters took me to their hearts when they came to realise I was one of them. They seemed to appreciate I was loyal and committed, and could be trusted to give everything. I was prepared to roll up my sleeves and scrap for the cause.

I am 5ft 9in tall but every time I pulled on my shirt and looked down at the badge on my chest, it made me feel like a giant. I am proud of everything I managed to achieve as a footballer. As I reflect I think I got the most from my talent, although I know I retired too soon because I never wanted to play for any other club.

It was always Southampton or nothing for me and here I was trying to visualise the final day of the Iron Fran challenge, the homecoming leg, carefully planned to coincide with the city's Marathon, in the hope it might give me the strength to keep going.

The unswerving support of family and so many friends and volunteers has helped me to reach this stage and I am a mere 50 miles away, at the Holiday Inn Hotel in Farnborough. Still, the finishing line seems a long way off.

Day Four, cycling through the hills on the way out of Bristol has taken such an incredible effort and my vision was failing. I was unable to focus on the device on my wrist with its digital display to show me how many miles there were to go and how quickly I was moving.

There were times when I simply did not have the energy to pick up my feet and mount the kerb during the marathon stage of the triathlon. We started in the morning with a 2.4-mile swim, followed by 112-mile bike ride and then onto the marathon run.

I am weaving around on the pavements like a drunk. Karen could not bear to watch. She knows I have been finding it increasingly difficult to consume the calories needed to sustain me. I am sleeping less than five hours at night. I am becoming increasingly weak and there are still three more days to go.

Alarm bells are ringing in my support team. I can tell Karen and my children, Luke and Kenzie, are worried and my physio Kelly goes through some routine checks before deciding to whisk me off for a more in-depth examination at the hospital.

Kelly fears my body is shutting down. We climb into a car and drive to Southampton General Hospital where the medics perform a series of tests on my heart, lungs and kidneys. They tell me my body is in urgent need of some rest, which makes sense, but, to everyone's surprise, they tell me all the clinical tests – my heart scan, and blood tests to determine my electrolyte levels – are clear.

I must have looked so tired and broken that they were expecting to find cardiac damage and they warn me that if I fail to take the advice to rest I will be risking permanent damage to my vital organs, not to mention my mental health.

My mind is usually strong. It is accustomed to those moments when the doubts wriggle in. I have been able to conquer them during the course of my football career and two of these ultra-endurance challenges. I struggled through an emotional breakdown on the first challenge in 2014, when I ran to each of the 20 Premier League grounds and covered more than 800 miles in three weeks.

Two years later, I added cycling to the running and set off to call at the 44 football grounds of the teams in the Premier League and Championship in the space of a fortnight. This was a challenge plagued by injury, in particular an Achilles tendon problem. One night, I woke to find it would no longer hold my body weight. My ankle simply gave way. I crawled across the floor of the hotel room to the bathroom and longed to give up. A few hours later, I was back on my feet running a marathon and cycling more than 100 miles into London.

If there has been one lesson to take from all of this, it concerns the power of the mind. The mind is strong enough to overcome perceptions of what the body can achieve. This time though, it does feel different and the warnings are rather severe.

I can see concern on the faces of those who love me, and who care about my health. I set out in search of something I thought might be impossible because I wanted to find my limits. To touch the very extremes of my physical capability. Perhaps I was there. Perhaps I had found them.

1

OH WHEN THE SAINTS...

'Francis Benali is a Southampton legend in more ways than one. I didn't know that was how it would work out when I knocked on the door of the family home and persuaded his mother he should sign for Saints. He was one of my last schoolboy signings. I don't think Franny ever wanted to play for anyone else. I signed him as a striker and he only ever scored one goal for the club so that goes to show my judgement.

To be truthful, his passing wasn't 100 per cent accurate either. The ball would finish up at the back of the stands as often as it would land at the feet of his teammates but he really could tackle. He had genuine tenacity and passion. He gave everything. He didn't mess around. I saw him dump wingers on the running track around the pitch.

The supporters loved him for that and, over time, he became one of their favourites. They had grown up with him. He was one of them. He loved the club. He was loyal. He gave everything. Off the pitch, he was one of the quietest, nicest lads you would ever wish to meet. On the pitch, once his lights switched on, look out.'

Lawrie McMenemy, Southampton manager 1973–85,
and director of football 1995–97

Very close to St Mary's Stadium, the home of Southampton Football, there is a block of flats called Albion Towers. These days it is clad in red and white in honour of the Saints, and if you are watching a game from the main stand and lift your eyes from the pitch, you will see it rising into the sky.

From a seat inside the ground, you could reach that tower block and the flat I once called home within just a few minutes. The quickest way is over the railway footbridge, now decorated with a montage of images and iconic photographs from the history of the club.

Look closely and you can find a couple of me in there – one of them shows me with my fists clenched in celebration and letting out a triumphant roar. We must have clinched some sort of crucial victory in one of our many successful fights against relegation.

It is unlikely I would have been celebrating a goal I scored. There were not many of those. In fact, only the one. I was more than happy to train my focus at the other end of the pitch and leave the glory to others.

Never in my wildest dreams did I imagine any of this when I was starting this journey on the Golden Grove estate, at the heart of St Mary's. Those were days before the football club had returned to its roots in this part of Southampton.

It was a bustling community, alive with industry and trade. I lived in a two-bed flat on the first floor of Albion Towers with my mother Mary and my grandfather Don. The view from our window looked out across the railway tracks, always busy with trains making their way to and from the docks.

Mum was small in stature but a big character. She always lived life to the full. She liked to party, enjoyed a drink and worked hard in different jobs when I was young. She worked at a taxi company in St Mary's for a time, and she was a cleaner, which often meant late nights. When I was older, she went to sea with Townsend Thoresen on the cross-Channel ferries, working on a shift pattern that meant she might be away for two weeks at a time.

My father, Billy, worked at sea for much of his working life. He was always immaculately dressed, usually in a tie with a handkerchief in the pocket of his jacket. His shoes were highly polished and shone like new and he slicked back his hair. Nothing out of place. He didn't have to be going off anywhere special to look as though he had just stepped from a shop window. He was a chef for Cunard on the QE2 for a time, and various other ships over the years. That's when he met my mum. They adopted me as a baby and then split up very soon afterwards.

Dad moved back to his native Liverpool and later remarried. This unusual family background did make me feel a little bit different. I was aware I didn't have the perfect family unit. Mum didn't earn a lot, I was on free school meals, and I would have permission to be pulled out of class once in a while to spend an hour or two with my dad, when he was ashore in Southampton between ships. Mum would dress me up smart when I went off to see him. It felt like a bit of a ceremony and not very natural. I was happier in a T-shirt and shorts.

My grandad Don was a foundling, abandoned by his parents when he was a baby. He was deaf and did not speak a word in his life. It would upset me as a young boy. I learned basic sign language from a young age so we were able to communicate. He was a kind, gentle man who resembled Andy Capp, the comic strip character from the *Mirror* newspaper. He never looked any different. Always wearing a flat cap and often smoking a cigarette. He enjoyed playing darts down at the pub, and loved watching all sports on the television.

We shared a bedroom when I was young and we formed a close bond. He was always keen to find out how I was getting on when I competed and proud as punch when I did well, maybe by winning a race in athletics or scoring a few goals. He passed away in 2001.

Life as an only child with Mum and Grandad in Southampton was radically different to time spent in Liverpool visiting my dad. I was the nephew or cousin rarely seen, and being such a big family, they all made

3

a fuss over me. I might have Christmas with them one year and the next year with my mum and grandad.

I can vividly recall kicking a ball about in the Liverpool streets with my cousins, and we stood on the Kop at Anfield and watched as Liverpool FC became the best team in the country and one of the best in the world under Bill Shankly and Bob Paisley.

My eldest cousin Paul would post clippings to me from newspapers and magazines. Kenny Dalglish was my favourite player. It meant I always had a firm allegiance to Liverpool, they were a side I liked and admired, but in reality Southampton were always my team. And these were exciting times at The Dell under Lawrie McMenemy. I would stand with mates in the Archers Road terrace or under the West Stand. Sometimes we would try to sneak in past the stewards at half time when people were coming out for a smoke, or go in for the last 15 minutes when they opened the gates to let fans out early.

The first game I saw under lights always stuck in my mind. I was completely mesmerised by the atmosphere. It was against West Brom, with Alan Ball and Kevin Keegan playing for Saints in the kit made by Patrick. Lawrie brought some big name stars to the club and I must have been one of very few boys playing football in Southampton not wearing the Patrick boots we called 'Keegan Kids' on their feet.

I was seven years old when we won the FA Cup in 1976. Our sitting room was quite a big room and it was packed for the big Wembley occasion. Communities seemed to be a bit closer back then. People were sitting on the floor and the drink was flowing. My grandad was there with a few cans of beer and I was in front of the TV, glued to the screen. I'm not sure I fully understood the magnitude of it all but it was exciting. The room erupted when Bobby Stokes ran clear to score the winner with only seven minutes to go. People were jumping around and hugging. I didn't know much about Bobby Stokes at the time but that changed once he scored the goal.

By this time, we had moved from the flat in St Mary's to rent a house in the Portswood area of the city. The building was almost derelict when we moved in. There was nothing on the floors. I'm not even sure there was a working kitchen. Mum put in a lot of hard work to decorate and make it a nice place to live. There was more space than we had in the flat although I was still sharing a bedroom with my grandad.

Mum grew tomatoes in a pot in the back garden. One day, probably looking to relieve my boredom, I decided to pull out the bamboo cane and picked some tomatoes, which weren't very ripe. I forced one of them onto the cane and flung it as far as I could. This worked well and I flung a few more in different directions. I wondered if I could fling one over the house. I was quite chuffed when I did it. Brilliant, I thought. I spotted Mum at the kitchen window and shouted out, 'Hey Mum, watch this.' I stuck another big green tomato on the cane, flung it as hard as I could and watched in horror as it crashed straight through the window to the side of where my mum was standing. I was out of there. Leapfrogged the garden wall and was gone. I did not hang around, I would have had a clip around the ear.

* * *

I was a pupil at Banister School, only a few yards from The Dell. I don't know where the idea came from, but I was convinced Lawrie and the team would drive by the school gates on Monday, parading the FA Cup in an open-top bus. Someone must have said something about it and I obviously misunderstood but I had my eyes peeled all day, looking out of the window during lessons (our classroom was at the front of the school) and craning my neck to see down the street during break. The kids were all buzzing about the FA Cup Final. I was disappointed when the parade I imagined never materialised.

When I moved up to middle school at St Mark's, my daily walk to school and back took me down Archers Road, right past The Dell. It was such an iconic ground in the 1980s. The four square sets of floodlights across the top of the East and West Stands were unique. It was such a tight configuration that the road running at an angle behind the Milton Road end made it seem as though there was a slice of the stand missing.

Without fail, I would stop at the old gates on Archers Road. They were large wooden gates, painted red, and there was a gap between them just wide enough to peer through and see a sliver of the pitch and, beyond the glistening surface, the Milton Road end of the stadium. I always thought I might catch a glimpse of a player or even see the team training. I never did. Saints actually trained elsewhere, but I would stand there and imagine life as a professional footballer.

There was not a lot of football on TV in those days, apart from Match of the Day on a Saturday night. I would pass hours of my spare time kicking a ball against the big wooden doors and metal shutters of a car dealership and a garage on our street or I would be down by the docks with friends, where there was a large play area. We swam in the outdoor lido in summer or paddled down the runway ramps and splashed about in the sea near to where the cruise liners docked. Health and safety might have something to say about that nowadays, but it was a fun place to be.

Southampton was the bustling port and the ships dominated the skyline in those areas. To see the QE2 sailing in was fantastic. A beautiful, distinctive ocean liner, instantly recognisable. My dad often worked on the QE2 so I would occasionally go down to see him off or to welcome the ship home.

Other times, we would head for Southampton Common where there was a paddling pool and we liked to kick a ball around on a small patch of grass close to the zoo, which has since closed. There were elephants in a tiny enclosure, penguins and a chimpanzee called James who blew raspberries and smoked cigarettes. Our goals would fly in accompanied by the roars of a nearby lion.

A teacher at St Mark's called John Ring was the first to recognise my qualities as an athlete, and used sport to inspire and encourage me. He was a classic schoolteacher of the age. He wore tweed trousers and brown brogues, and the hard soles of his shoes echoed down the corridor and told you he was on his way before you saw him. His inspiration came in the form of how he made me feel, rather than what he said. He brought out my best by challenging me, such as dividing boys into teams with me on the weaker side.

I was not very academic. One of my school reports states I was 'an erratic worker' with a 'rather indifferent attitude' and 'easily distracted'. I would get lost very quickly in classes. If you didn't keep up you were left behind, and I was left behind but I never said anything and things went from bad to worse. There were some exams when it hardly seemed worth picking up the pen. I just didn't have a clue.

I lived for PE or break time and the chance to kick a ball around in the playground. I was big, physically mature, strong and fast. Most of the positive reports at school would relate to PE. 'Alert and active' said one, 'a natural ball player' and 'outstanding in terms of attitude and performance'. That was more like it. I did well on sports day. I knew I was quite good.

I was always quick and a good sprinter despite no formal athletics training. I was a county schools champion at the hurdles when I moved up to Bellemoor School, an all-boys school at the time and now called Upper Shirley High. The record stood for many years. It might even still be standing!

I played some rugby and was a decent bowler when it came to cricket, but football was where I excelled and where my true passion lay. Even so, I didn't play for an organised club until I was 13 years old – the opportunity just didn't present itself. Once, I cycled across Southampton for a trial only to find no one there. I don't know how it happened. There must've been a communication breakdown. I was cheesed-off to say the least.

At 13, I was invited to join Windsor United after doing well in a five-a-side competition at school. Windsor played in the Southampton Tyro League, in Totton, and I would get a lift with the parents of other boys in the team. I was used to it.

Colin Harris, the father of Mark, a school friend, was very kind and often ferried me around to various football and cricket matches. Colin would also put together a five-a-side 'Dream Team' with the best players we knew and, in the summer months, drive us to tournaments all over Hampshire and Dorset in his Ford Granada. That was always great fun and we would frequently win and leave with the trophy.

I started out on the left wing and was immediately banging in the goals. They converted me to a striker and it all seemed to go very well, with me scoring at will. I was so much bigger than the other boys and the beginnings of the moustache scared the life out of opponents. There's an old team photo from school where I was in the front row, surrounded by lads of the same age from my secondary school and I look like one of the teachers. I didn't think too much about it at the time. It wasn't a conscious decision to grow a moustache. It just sort of appeared and I left it there – for quite a long time.

The parents of the opposition players would complain about me, saying I was clearly too old to be in this age group and direct abuse at me. I probably trampled straight over a few of the smaller kids, not with any deliberate intent of course, but it would rile the parents. I'd knocked little Johnny to the floor and scored three or four goals. I was the target for their comments and it wasn't pleasant. I felt intimidated by the parents and managers, grown men. Sometimes I felt threatened, not in every game, but frequently and I had to stand up to that by myself. I didn't have family with me on the touchline, saying, 'Just ignore it Franny' or going over to have a word on my behalf. I was there with a team but I felt isolated and on my own, occasionally to the point where I'd be thinking that I'd have to have my wits about me at the end of the game.

Very quickly, I had to develop a tough skin and stand up for myself, an attitude that would come in handy during my professional career.

At 13, I was playing for Southampton Schoolboys in the final of a county tournament against Poole. We played at The Dell straight after a first-team game. This was a big deal. It was my job to introduce the team to

Kevin Keegan and I still have the photograph. I scored twice, set up another goal and we won the trophy. It was like a dream, more because of the fact that we were on the pitch I had always dreamed of playing on, I had met Keegan and there were what felt like lots of supporters watching, maybe a couple of hundred. For some reason, the shape of the goalposts at The Dell stuck in my mind. They seemed to be unique. Not round or square, but oval-shaped posts and the netting was pegged down vertically from the stanchion, quite tight to the posts, not stretched out at an angle behind because there wasn't room. The terrace was so close. The net was like a box. To me, it seemed like a posh goal and I was thrilled to score a couple.

After this performance, Southampton invited me to go down to The Dell and train a couple of nights a week with some other lads of similar ages the club were looking at and thinking of signing up on associate schoolboy forms. I walked to the ground, and we changed in the visitors' dressing room. These were my first encounters with Bob Higgins, the club's youth development officer, who had great influence when it came to which young players were signed up. Bob took the sessions in the old gym behind the main stand. We called it a gym even though it was nothing more than a huge room made of breeze blocks with a couple of fire doors in one corner and goals of different sizes painted on the walls. It was noisy as the sounds bounced off the bare walls.

There was a polished wooden floor covered in markings supposed to help the goalkeepers with their angles. It was basic, certainly not the modern 3G or 4G training facilities Premier League teams have today, and it had a real chill in winter. Sometimes it seemed colder than it was outside.

* * *

Life really changed when Lawrie McMenemy knocked on our front door. There were a few clubs showing interest in me. I had letters from Arsenal and Aston Villa, inviting me along for trials, and Portsmouth, down the road, were interested, but Lawrie knew I was a big Saints fan. I did not want to sign anywhere else.

He turned up on the doorstep, more than anything to reinforce the idea with my mum. This was how he ran the club. He was the first-team manager and a huge personality in English football at the time. He took a close interest in what was going on at every level of the club, and approved all the schoolboy signings.

To have him dropping in on the family home in Portswood was a big deal. We scrambled around tidying up cushions and Mum was bringing out the best china. It was all very surreal to think the Saints boss was in the living room. They had a cuppa and a conversation and I sat in the room, listening. It was great to hear how much Lawrie wanted me. 'Southampton is the right club for your son to learn his trade as a footballer,' he was saying. 'To grow as a person, and he will get opportunities.'

Football was never Mum's thing. She never tried to lead me one way or the other where my career was concerned, but it went a long way for her to see Lawrie had made the effort to visit and chat to us. So I signed schoolboy forms at 14. This was my first official connection with Southampton and I was now part of the club, pulling on the red-and-white shirt and representing Saints. It meant the world to me, not least because I was now on the next rung of the ladder, still at school but making progress towards where I wanted to be. I was like a sponge, determined to soak up everything and work towards proving that I was worth taking on a youth training scheme (YTS) at the age of 16.

To continue successfully along this path, I would have to impress the club's coaching staff, including Bob Higgins, who would be our head coach for the next two years. To make the next step, I would have to perform well in his team. Bob certainly revelled in his reputation as a star-maker and I followed the case very closely in the media when, in 2019, he was found guilty of 45 counts of indecent assault on schoolboy footballers over a period of 25 years, from 1971 to 1996. I wasn't required to attend court as a witness but the police came to interview me during the process and took down a statement. I told them everything I knew, which was that I had become aware of rumours among young players once I signed as a trainee. Sometimes opposition players would say, 'Bob's this you know, and Bob's that.' I guess I didn't want to believe it at the time, and the first time anything was made public about his criminal activity was when Dean Radford and five other young players made official complaints to the police. The case went to a trial in 1989 and a lot of information came out. Dean was someone I knew. He was slightly younger than I was, and it must have been incredibly tough for him to open up on this.

I never experienced anything directly with Bob. Not on a one-to-one basis. I was the local lad, living at home with my mum. I didn't stay overnight on the residential camps like some of the others. I'd travel home at the end of the day and go back the next morning. I wasn't sleeping in the dorms like a lot of the lads who travelled from around the country.

The only time I experienced anything I can say was unusual came on a trip to Sweden when I was about 14. At the time it felt very uncomfortable and looking back now, more fully aware of everything, it was obviously very wrong. We were playing in a well-established youth tournament called the Gothia Cup, which still takes place annually, in Gothenburg, and involves teams from all over the world. It was a brilliant event. The city was abuzz with thousands of young players.

We were there with a Saints side and Bob was in charge. We were sleeping in a school hall on inflatable beds and part of our pre-match preparation and post-match recovery was to have a soap-water massage. This wasn't a one-to-one scenario, we weren't alone in a room. There were benches out around the hall and other staff members were present but we were naked when we had these massages.

We did not keep a pair of shorts on, or even our pants. We were told to strip because that was how the pros did it. I can remember feeling very uneasy about it at the time. I was embarrassed and I was embarrassed for the other lads. But I was aspiring to be a professional footballer and apparently this was something we were expected to do. I really didn't know any different. As a teenager you don't really speak out. You are still a child, trying not to speak out of turn. Over time, a few of the lads would mention these things quietly among ourselves – not to the staff – but we moved on, even though inwardly I don't think any of us were comfortable with it. It was a competitive environment and we were focused on being taken on as YTS apprentices.

Bob was in such an influential position. He held so many people's futures in his hand. It is clear now there were other levels of abuse going on behind the scenes. Abuse is abuse and there can be no excuses – what happened was totally unacceptable. My heart goes out to those teammates who were caught up in it. And there is an element of guilt. When I look back on it from my perspective as an adult and a father, it is heartbreaking. To have been put through such trauma must have been horrendous.

Sometimes I wonder if there were signs and I missed them, or if there was something I might have done differently at the time. To say it was 'laughed about' or 'joked about' would be wrong but it was quickly played down whenever the issue cropped up. On those occasions when we talked about it as a group, maybe there were some boys reaching out, looking for support or to find someone else who had witnessed the same things. Maybe those were the signs I could have picked up on but I didn't know how deeply affected any of the individuals were or what they were going through.

Bob Higgins left Southampton after the court case in 1989, although he wasn't convicted at the time. He was acquitted of one case and the others were discontinued, and it would be another 30 years before his crimes were punished. He sexually abused boys, most of them in his care during his time at Southampton and in a similar role at Peterborough United. In June 2019, at the age of 66, he was finally jailed for 24 years.

I am pleased for those players who have been able to find justice. I hope it has brought some degree of closure. It must have been terrible to go through what they did, to live with it for so long, to go through it again in court and to go on living with it.

* * *

When I joined Southampton's Schoolboy ranks, my footballing career seemed to accelerate. Please remember that I was not playing football in an organised team until I was 13, which was unusual at the time and even less common in the modern game, when the top clubs bring the most promising players into their academy systems at the age of six or seven. Then there was the Cup Final at The Dell and, at 14, I was signing for Saints. At 15, I was selected for England Schoolboys. It was the pinnacle, an incredible honour to be chosen to represent my country as a centre-forward, with the lions on my chest and a number nine on my back.

I was flying. I had belief and confidence. I scored on my England debut, against Northern Ireland at Scarborough, in March 1984. It was the only goal of the game, a free-kick on the edge of the box, with my left foot. It would be nice to claim the sort of swerving technique you see from David Beckham or James Ward-Prowse. In truth, it was more about brute force, driven low and firm.

There were some good players in that team. A couple of them went on to have long careers in the game, such as Mark Burke who started at Aston Villa and went on to play for Middlesbrough and Wolves, and Gareth Hall who played for Chelsea. But then there were others highly tipped to be the next big thing who did not go on to play professionally.

I scored three goals in nine appearances for England, the most memorable of them a goal at the Olympic Stadium in Berlin against West Germany, in April. About 60,000 spectators came to watch, with lots of British troops with Union flags inside the ground. Unfortunately, they saw us get thumped 4-1 by the Germans, a technical and well-drilled team, on another level to us. They beat us twice on that trip but it was a great education to visit the Cold War's divided city, and see the Berlin Wall and its military checkpoints.

We also played at Wembley against Netherlands and Scotland, and my family and friends hired a coach to take them to the game to support me. I tried to savour the occasion, the walk out of the huge Wembley dressing room, up the concrete slope, and out of the old tunnel behind the goal. The sight of the packed crowd and explosion of noise sent a tingle down my back. I could picture the FA Cup Finals and internationals I had watched on TV as a boy. Before the first of the games, I was handed a telegram sent by Southampton striker Frank Worthington, which was a lovely touch and meant a lot. We won both games, but as a striker I was quite disappointed not to score any goals.

I still have my England kit and the cap (just the one cap, not one for each game), and some memorabilia, which is nice to look back on. I also tried to keep programmes and some reports and photos from the local newspaper from my schoolboy football days. I seemed to get a fair bit of positive coverage. I also have a letter from Southampton, dated 14 May, 1985 and signed by Lawrie, inviting me onto the YTS at the club, to begin on 1 July.

* * *

I was 16 and would be paid £26.50 a week. We collected wages every Friday afternoon from the reception at The Dell. It came in cash with a pay slip in a little brown envelope, with a bonus of £2 if the youth team had drawn, or £4 for a win. A few wins could boost your earnings. We also got a bus pass to get to and from the ground and into town on our day release for college, where we studied for a sport and leisure qualification. We learned some first aid. In the nicest possible way, the guys viewed it as a day off and a chance to recover.

I was physically and mentally shattered from the step up to full-time work. It was a shock to the system after previously only training a couple of times a week and playing a few games. Not only did we have the daily exertion of training and working hard on our football, we had other jobs off the pitch, too.

We were expected to be at the club early to go into the laundry and get your designated pro's kit. George Lawrence was my pro. George was a winger who, like me, came through the Saints youth system and moved to Oxford for three years before returning to The Dell.

We polished boots, pumped up balls and loaded the van to take all the kit to the training ground where we'd set up the pitches with cones for the sessions. After training, we'd take everything back to the stadium, clean dressing rooms and the bathrooms, and do odd jobs around the ground.

Often there was an afternoon session or a gym session. I would go home, in the early weeks, collapse on the sofa and fall asleep, but I loved every second of it and was determined to make the most of this opportunity.

* * *

Dave Merrington was our youth team coach. Dave was a Geordie who used to play for Burnley. After retiring as a player he worked as a probation officer. He was tough on us, setting standards both on and off the pitch.

Every day we stood and waited as he checked the quality of our work, running his finger along ledges to check for dust. If something wasn't to his liking we'd all stay until it was. He was preparing us for life, not just for football and that grounding rubbed off on us all. We had a talented crop of players and some real characters. Matt Le Tissier, Allen

Tankard, Steve Davis and Keith Granger were among those in my YTS intake.

The year above ours included Phil Parkinson, Mark Blake, Ian Hamilton and Chris Wilder. In the year below were Rod and Ray Wallace, Neil Maddison and Alan Shearer. I followed all their careers with great interest when they moved on as players and, in some cases such as Phil and Chris, became successful managers. It is always nice to bump into them and catch up.

The scouting network was good at drawing in lads like Shearer and Maddison from the North-East, and the Wallaces and Steve Williams from London. There was a history of Scottish players going back to the days when Ted Bates was the manager in the 1960s, as well as players from the West Country and Wales. It was an advanced process for its time.

Dave would take us to visit places like the Ford Transit factory where he wanted to show us people working shifts in the real world and open our eyes to something other than football, and to help us appreciate the opportunity we'd been given. It was important for young footballers. I was impressed when I read about Marcelo Bielsa taking his squad out on litter-picking duties when he arrived at Leeds years later in 2018. It does build character. I know the impact Dave's life lessons had on me.

We went down to a local shelter for recovering alcoholics and addicts and we'd sit and chat to them, and join them each year for a Christmas dinner. With my upbringing, I did not need reminding that football did not resemble the real world. I knew I was fortunate but this reinforced it and was the time I started to understand why it was important for a football club to put something back into its community.

Years later when Matt Le Tissier was the team captain and I was the club captain we made it our business to support good causes and we've always continued to do that. It has been the driving force behind all the fundraising challenges I've done.

People are all different but collectively I always thought there was a Southampton stamp on the players who came through those youth ranks at the time. Without doubt, it came from Dave Merrington and it went beyond what happened on the pitch. I am certain it is a major reason why so many of those players went on to thrive in and out of the game.

* * *

There were some big characters in the first-team dressing room, lots of whom I admired from a distance. Then suddenly, I was thrown into the same environment as them. Many were international footballers and household names including Peter Shilton, Mark Dennis, Jimmy Case, David Armstrong, Joe Jordan, Mark Wright, Nick Holmes and Danny Wallace. They had finished as runners-up in Division One in 1984, the club's best-ever finish in the league. In 1985, they finished fifth and Lawrie was tempted back to his native North-East to become manager of Sunderland. His departure was huge news in Southampton. He had been in charge for almost 12 years, ever since I had been watching football, and before I could report for my first day as an apprentice he was gone. That was disappointing but it didn't detract from my overall excitement. His successor was Chris Nicholl. He was a genuine guy and a former player under Lawrie. Chris knew how the club ticked.

Shilts was a big presence at the time. He was very much his own man. In those days before goalkeeping coaches were considered to be integral members of the staff he took all the goalkeepers, right the way down the ranks to the apprentices, to train with him.

Nick Holmes was someone who had always been at Southampton. He played in the FA Cup Final in 1976 and the League Cup Final in 1979. He was a solid pro and a lovely man. He had such a quiet nature off the pitch and was someone I have always respected. He was willing to share his knowledge, and I tried to behave in that way when I reached the same stage of my career. Many years later, he tried to sign me when he was manager of Salisbury.

To be training with Jimmy Case was quite surreal. Jimmy used to live just around the corner from my dad in the Macket's Lane area of Liverpool. I would take my ball and kick it around in the streets near his house. I remembered following Jimmy as a player. He was tough as nails, a fabulous footballer and a true champion. In eight years at Liverpool, he won the league title four times, the European Cup three times and all sorts of major honours. It was a sensational career and he was a big influence on and off the pitch at Southampton.

It could be quite intimidating for a 16-year-old and you knew your place. Maybe they'd been through a similar journey. Maybe it was even tougher in their day. They certainly weren't throwing their arms open wide and welcoming you in.

If you went into the first-team dressing room to make tea or put out kit, you did your job and got straight out. A pair of boots might be thrown in your direction and you would be told to 'get them cleaned'.

There was no hanging around, chatting with the senior players. You had to earn your right to be in there and earn their respect through your conduct and your football. As youth team players, we did mix with the first team during training. We'd be drafted in if the manager needed extra players to put on a certain session.

Chris Nicholl, an imposing centre-half in his playing days, was still young and fit enough to join in training games. I was a striker and he was a defender, and I'd often come up against him and he'd be kicking lumps out of me.

Every bone in my body wanted to fight back but this was the manager. He was a good person but also a fierce competitor. I had seen him almost come to blows in the dressing room with Mark Dennis. Mark was a talented left-back, affectionately known as 'Psycho' because of the wild side to his nature, and there had been simmering tension between them when it all erupted after a match. Mark moved to QPR not long afterwards.

What was I supposed to do when Chris was kicking me in a five-a-side? I think he wanted to see if I could be bullied or if I was going to stand up for myself. I had to pass a few tests, like all the lads.

* * *

On match days, we worked with the rest of the staff behind the scenes. We saw at close quarters the preparation and build up for a game, saw how the pros got ready, watched the crowd coming in, and felt the buzz and anticipation. The atmosphere was incredible. I wanted to be part of this. The smell of the muscle oils and Deep Heat. I was mesmerised by it all.

The visiting teams arrived and I marvelled at some of the big stars of the era. Some players were bigger than you expected, some were smaller. West Ham captain Billy Bonds strolled past me and in the corridor wearing just his shorts and socks. 'Blimey,' I thought, 'What an incredible physique.' Bonds was approaching the end of his career and he was on his way to a pre-match chat with the referee. That was something else I didn't know about, the players went to chat with the referee. I was hanging around with my bucket and mop. No one told me to clear off. I was there to do a job, visible in case the visiting team needed an errand running, although I was clearly eavesdropping. I wanted to hear it all, if there was an ear-bashing from the manager or an argument between players.

After games, there were opportunities to get inside and start cleaning when some of the players were still there. I was curious to understand what went on. How did other teams go about things? How did their players interact? What were they talking about? I listened to their conversations about the game.

Nottingham Forest came to The Dell and lost one year in December and I was outside their dressing room when their manager, Brian

Clough, was getting ready to leave. He wasn't in the best of moods as he motioned for me to go inside and start my cleaning. He wandered off and I said to him, 'Merry Christmas Mr Clough'. He disappeared without responding. Then, a few seconds later, he poked his head back round the door and said, 'And a Merry Christmas to you, young man.' I was chuffed to bits.

The reserves played in the Football Combination, a now-defunct league competition for reserve teams in the south of England. I was 16 and still at school when I made my first appearance in the Combination as a substitute against Fulham and, yet, I could be on the pitch with a senior pro who had 300 games under his belt. That was crazily tough schooling, but it was great because you had to stand up and be counted or you would fall by the wayside. Some would argue it was not the right way but there were a lot of good things to take from it.

I came up against Scotland international Charlie Nicholas playing for the reserves. He was at Arsenal, who paid £750,000 to sign him from Celtic a few years earlier. It was a big transfer at the time. I was still a teenage striker and it gave me a real lift to see a name like that on the teamsheet ahead of a game. You were up against high-profile players and played in major stadiums. Modern football has changed a lot for the better since my days, but the levels in reserve team football have gone backwards. Back then, reserve team football was a lot closer to the first-team game and far more competitive. It attracted a reasonable crowd and was more physical. By the time you made it through the Combination and reserve-team football, you were fully accustomed to going to famous venues and coming up against household names.

By the time I broke into the senior team, early in the 1988–89 season, I was beyond the stage where I might be awestruck by the heroes I admired at school. I never put an opponent on a pedestal. I always saw it as a level playing field. They might have been more talented but I couldn't view it that way.

Things were getting more serious. Chris Nicholl would be up in the stands watching the reserve team play and we all knew he wasn't afraid to call a young player into the first team squad. That was always an incentive. After training every Friday, at The Dell, the weekend squad lists for the youth team, the reserves and the first team were pinned to the noticeboard in the home dressing room. Everyone would go in to scan the lists. Depending on the stage of your development you might be scanning all three sheets, hoping for the best outcome. Were you joining the youth team for an early start for a trip to Colchester, sitting on the skips, the enormous storage baskets we used to transport kit in those days, in the back of a minibus? Or were you in the first team squad?

* * *

Matt Le Tissier was one of the first in our age group to be called up by Chris. He more or less bypassed the reserve team, went into the first team and never really came back.

Matt's path ran parallel to my own but was really quite different. He came from a large, close-knit family in Guernsey. His brother Karl had been to Southampton on trial and missed his family and friends and life on the island. He didn't make the transition so it must have been a huge step for Matt to move away and live with a host family in Millbrook, a suburb of the city.

We struck up a friendship from the start. He was a likeable guy, quiet but confident and one of those annoying people who could turn their hand to anything when it came to sport. Whether it was golf or snooker he always seemed to be really good. His general knowledge is also incredible and he's good with numbers, winning a number of *Countdown* shows.

Once, we represented Southampton on a TV quiz competition and my son Luke came along to the studios. We were on the way home when Luke said, 'Dad, did you get paid for that?' and I said, 'Yeah, there's a few quid in it'. Luke joked, 'What, even though Matt answered every question?' He definitely had a good point.

Matt and I joined Southampton as trainees, we were teammates, in the same year group and the same youth team, and our bond strengthened as each season went by with players leaving the club. Eventually we were the only ones remaining, the last two with that connection. Our history was a shared history on the pitch and at the training ground and that deepened our friendship even more.

I've always admired his ability. You could see immediately that he had something special. At first, I wasn't sure if this was the norm at this level and it was only as we moved up through the ranks and he was still performing that way in the first team that I realised he was in fact an absolute genius.

He was tall and thin in those early days and he drifted past players so easily. He was never blessed with too much pace but he could run a bit. And you had to run a bit in Dave Merrington's teams.

He took a lot of criticism because he didn't run around like others but it was unfair to brand him a lazy player. He may not have been as fast as some and he did not spend hours working on his physique in the gym but he never failed to do the preseason training runs and fitness work, or the training we did as a team, and he would devote so much time to perfecting his technique on his free-kicks, corners and penalties.

When the ball was at his feet he came to life. As a teammate, you trusted him in any scenario: any game, any venue, any environment. You gave him the ball and he would look after it. More than that, he would do something useful with it and often he would produce that bit of magic out of nowhere.

There were loads of examples of this and I count myself fortunate to have seen him play football every single day on the training ground. Some of the things he did in training were even more spectacular than those he did in games – outrageous flicks and volleys, long-range efforts and pin-point set-pieces targeting a small area of the net, and all made to look effortless.

Other players would be standing there, with mouths open at his sheer audacity, and would just start clapping. What amazed me most was that as a fellow pro and a teammate I would still be thinking, how do you actually do that?

I knew him so well and I could detect the signs from his body shape and attempts at disguise and I almost always knew what he was going to do next. I could be playing in a little training game against him, I would see the sign and know what he was going to do and I still couldn't stop him. The most infuriating thing was when he would nutmeg someone and laugh afterwards. That used to drive me bonkers. So of course I admired his ability as a footballer. I also liked his character and his quick wit.

We struggled in the Premier League for so many years and plenty of opportunities cropped up for him to go elsewhere but Matt was very happy at Saints and had no desire to leave. He was the star player in our side and he enjoyed that.

I never wanted him to go. I knew how important he was for us – and if he had moved I might have had to kick him – but there's a small part of me that would have liked to have seen what he could have achieved at a top team like Manchester United, surrounded by world-class players.

He did it here with us at Southampton and we didn't have the same calibre of players. The dynamics would have been different, he might have had to commit more defensively, but in terms of talent he would have easily fitted in.

I'm pleased he stayed and his sense of loyalty only strengthened my love for him and over the years he became my best pal. I enjoy his company. We enjoy reminiscing, although his memory is better than mine. He's fun to be around. Our families have shared many happy memories over the years. Karen and I are godparents to his daughter, Ava. We even look after each other's dogs when we are away on holidays.

There's no question he would have enjoyed the sort of recognition his talent deserved had he played for a club regularly challenging for silverware. It would have benefited his international prospects and probably earned him more money.

England had some big players at the time, such as Paul Gascoigne. Even so, I knew what Matt could do for us as a team. I was always gobsmacked when he was overlooked by the national team.

In some ways he was an easy target and a bit of a scapegoat. It became easier to leave him out than to pick him. It's such a shame a lot of England managers didn't look at what he was doing quite literally every week for Southampton. It's not as if he did these incredible things once or twice. It was week in and week out, season in and season out.

I have no doubt he could have done it. He was producing it regularly against world-class teams and world-class defenders. Given our history in penalty shoot-outs I would have taken Matt along to the World Cup or the Euros even if it was only as a dead-ball specialist.

His ability to take penalties and free-kicks was as good as anybody I can ever remember seeing. He would even shoot from corners. He had the ability and the confidence. He whipped the ball in at such pace and such a height that it could take a deflection off a defender and go in. Some of the stuff was outrageous. As his teammate, I would be prepared to run any distance or do any amount of physical work, running, tackling and heading in the knowledge I could give Matt the ball to score us a goal.

You would never get on his back and give him grief for not tracking back. You might say, 'Come on mate, get back in a defensive position now and again' and, if you said that, he was very willing. But you wouldn't want him wasted in those defensive areas because he had a sixth sense of where to be on the football pitch.

He is adored by everyone at Southampton and rightly so. As a player he's the best I played with for sure, without hesitation. I treasure his friendship and it was an absolute joy to play in the same team as him for all those years.

2

...GO MARCHING IN

'Franny walked into the football club like a man. He already had the little moustache. He wasn't blessed with the talent of Matt Le Tissier or Alan Shearer but he was a very good player and he had natural aggression, determination and mental toughness. No one liked playing against him.

He was a one-off, a great character and easy for a coach to handle. He worked on his game. He would do anything and play anywhere you asked. We had to control his aggression and channel it in the right direction. If you don't nail that early on it can become a problem.

He took it all on board but his progress wasn't always smooth. There was a spell when the crowd took a dislike to him and turned on him. He never let it get to him at all. If it did he didn't let it show. He always said he would win them over and he did. He battled through the odds. And they came to love him like they love Matt Le Tissier.'

Dave Merrington, former Southampton youth team
coach, and manager 1995–96

There was no negotiation over my first professional contract. I was asked to go and see Chris Nicholl, the manager, and he had something written on a piece of paper and he slid it across the desk. There it is. Those are the terms. No agents, no parents. It was £100 a week. Chris said, 'There's the pen or there's the door', and that was the extent of it.

He said it was the start, a recognition of where I was, and that if I continued improving and broke into the first team he promised we'd be able to sit down and renegotiate. That did happen. It wasn't a massive increase but he was true to his word and turning pro was the big thing. I signed on my 18th birthday, 30 December, 1986.

It was one of my proudest moments and an exciting time. We all knew Chris wasn't afraid to put the young players from the youth system into the first team. We still had senior players with countless games behind them, such as Jimmy Case, Russell Osman and Glenn Cockerill, but some of the younger boys were breaking through.

Alan Shearer and Matt Le Tissier had already made appearances and scored a few goals. Alan made quite an impact when he scored a hat-trick against Arsenal on his first start, when he was only 17. No mean feat when you consider the Arsenal back line and their reputation for defending under George Graham. I was thrilled for both Alan and Matt and it was a genuine motivation to see your youth teammates doing it on the big stage.

We had a good crop of talent. Rod and Ray Wallace broke through. Neil Ruddock, Jason Dodd and Tim Flowers came to the club when they were young. We played with a fearlessness and flair and, in later years, when we were fighting relegation, the unity and spirit helped us. A lot of us had been together for a long time.

My first opportunity arrived in October 1988, coming on as a substitute to replace Kevin Moore in a goalless draw against Derby, at The Dell. I'd played there countless times but usually against an empty backdrop when it was easy to see your teammates and the colour of their shirts in your peripheral vision. Suddenly, I found the place was full of supporters, most of them in red and white, and some literally a yard or two from the pitch. I really had to make sure the pass was going where I wanted. I had to adapt.

We had started the season with three wins and a creditable draw at Arsenal, overshadowed by a nasty injury for Glenn Cockerill. Glenn suffered a double fracture in his jaw after taking a punch from Paul Davis. It became a big story and Davis later received a nine-match ban.

I was 19 and playing in midfield at the time, midway through my transition from striker to defender. The positional change was at least partly to do with my inability to control my temperament once I crossed the white line and stepped onto the pitch. My disciplinary record had already taken a turn for the worse with a red card in the South East Counties Second Division League Cup Final against Crystal Palace, and numerous bookings. Dave Merrington and Chris Nicholl reached the conclusion it might suit my qualities as a footballer and a character if I moved into midfield rather than continue up in attack. They thought I might not be so easily wound-up if I was the one doing the marking – and therefore doing the kicking and holding – rather than the one being marked, kicked and held. I was always likely to start a battle if I came in for any rough treatment from the centre-halves.

Also, they probably looked at the talent we had coming through in the shape of Shearer, Le Tissier and Rod Wallace. It would have been quite a challenge for me to establish myself in the first team as a striker.

When I was scoring goals in my schoolboy days, a lot of my success was down to my size, power and speed. As I got older, during my apprenticeship years between 16 and 18, I began to find other guys catching up with me. In terms of size, quite a few of them were bigger than I was. I was still quick but it wasn't quite so easy to score the goals.

As a midfielder, I was far from being a Jimmy Case but I was aggressive and tenacious. I was prone to a mistake now and then, but I had a desire and a focus on the pitch. I was so driven to do well and win that I would overstep the mark on occasions. I hope that went some way to making me the opponent I was, and the teammate I was, especially when it was time to stand up and be counted in some of our relegation battles.

I made a third appearance from the bench in a 2–1 home defeat against Sheffield Wednesday. It was a game when Ray Wallace made his debut alongside his twin Rod and their elder brother Danny, and was the first time since the 1920s that any team in the Football League had included three brothers.

The three Wallaces were still in the team three days later when I made my full debut at Tottenham. I had played at White Hart Lane a number of times but all of a sudden this was first-team football, an evening game, under the lights and the stadium was full. To run out of the tunnel and experience the roar of the crowd was something else.

I was playing in midfield, up against Paul Gascoigne. Gazza could glide past you with what seemed to be little or no effort. He was deceptively strong and hard to shake from the ball. He was one of England's best players but I was determined to treat him like any other opponent.

When Alan Ball became Saints boss, a few years later, he shared the advice his father had given him before the World Cup finals in 1966, which was: 'If you're ever feeling overawed by one of your opponents, grab hold of him by the shorts and unless he has three of them down there, he's no more special than you.' Good advice, I thought.

We won 2–1 at Spurs and I stayed in the team for the next game against Norwich. It was a fantastic feeling to make the breakthrough, but I was soon dropped and by the end of the season looked back and had started only three games. The sense of disappointment was strong especially as we went through a long run without a win. I had tasted life in the first team and wanted more.

The following season brought a move from midfield to defence. The switch came almost by chance, as often is the case in football. It was 30 September, 1989, we were up against Wimbledon at home and short on left-backs. Derek Statham had just left us for Stoke and Micky Adams was out. Gerry Forrest had been switched over from right-back only to pick up an injury early in the game. Chris looked down the bench, saw me, a natural leftie, and said, 'Can you do us a job there today?' 'Yeah, definitely,' I shot back. I jumped at the chance. I had never played left-back before in my life but I must have done reasonably well because that was where I stayed. I slotted into the team, starting 23 league games as we finished seventh in Division One.

I was in my new full-back role when Liverpool came to visit The Dell in October. They were on top of the league and unbeaten. They had lost the title to Arsenal in a dramatic final match the previous season and they were determined to win it back, which they ended up doing.

With John Barnes, Ian Rush and Peter Beardsley, they were the team of the era and, on the day, we beat them 4–1 with a young team. It remained one of the most memorable games of my career, perhaps because of my family connection to Liverpool, and the fact that I had supported them as a boy, along with the Saints. For 90 minutes we were simply too good for them. Alan Shearer was up front with Paul Rideout, flanked by Matt Le Tissier and Rod Wallace. It seemed as though we would score every time we attacked.

It was a great time to be playing. We conceded a few but with this attacking formation we always scored goals. It was Rod's best season for Saints, scoring 21 goals in all competitions, with Matt our top scorer with 24. Matt won the PFA Young Player of the Year award with Rod in second. They, together with Alan, were drawing attention from wealthier clubs, especially as we beat Luton 6–3, scored four against QPR and Charlton, and scored eight in two games against Norwich.

* * *

I was soon feeling more comfortable as a full-back and the transition helped my career, but the creative side of my game was not as good as it should have been. Modern full-backs are expected to bomb forward, produce crosses and score goals but I was an out-and-out defender. I would try to keep things simple, protect our penalty area, supply the wide man in front of me or play the ball into midfield areas.

As an apprentice watching the first team, I would focus mostly on the strikers. When my position changed to midfield, I studied Jimmy Case. He was the senior player, the team captain and a leader. From the centre of midfield he would pull the strings of the whole team and I tried to learn the positions he would take up.

From an educational point of view I missed out on the chance to study top-class full-backs such as Mark Dennis and Derek Statham. Centre-halves like Russell Osman, Kevin Moore and Neil Ruddock were great, and they talked me through those early games. 'Stay here, tuck inside, push on,' I was always ready to listen and eager to learn from these class players. They knew how to manage a game and there was a lot of communication.

At no point in my career did I think I knew everything, or even knew my position. I always felt there was something more to learn from a teammate or a staff member or an opponent. I wanted to be the best I could be.

Rod Wallace often played in front of me in the early days, which was amazing. He was lightning fast, very much like his older brother Danny, who left Southampton for Manchester United in September 1989, and perhaps with more of an eye for goal.

Rod's electric pace scared defenders to death and he had good feet and good ability. He comes to my mind whenever I see Raheem Sterling. They were similar sorts of players. You could give him the ball in a tight situation and he would look after it.

He was always willing to come back and defend. Sometimes I'd have to tell him to leave me to do my job and save his legs for going forward, and that didn't happen too many times over the course of my career. More often, I'd be screaming at the wingers to get back and help me.

It was a real shame when Rod and his brother Ray left us to join Leeds United in the summer of 1991. Maybe Danny's transfer to United had a bearing on the decision and they didn't think Saints were big enough to fulfil their ambitions.

The move worked out well for them. The Wallace twins were champions at the end of their first season at Leeds. At Southampton, it felt as if we were breaking up something special, since they were good lads and we had come through the system together.

Twelve months later and Alan Shearer was sold to Blackburn for a British record transfer fee of £3.3million. His goals fired them to the Premier League title in 1995, with Tim Flowers in goal. This was a lot of top-class talent leaving our club at a young age. It would have been great to see what we could have gone on to achieve with Shearer, Flowers, Le Tissier and Rod Wallace together for a few more years. It was one of the real disappointments, thinking what might have been.

* * *

Of course Alan went on to become the greatest centre-forward of the modern era. His record of 260 goals in the Premier League will stand the test of time. It doesn't even include the goals he scored before he left Southampton in 1992. Just imagine how many goals he would have scored without missing so much playing time from serious knee injuries.

I was a striker in the youth team when he came into the club as an apprentice, a year after me. The powerful physique and strong mentality, the hallmarks of Al's career, were clearly evident at the age of 16.

Le Tissier's football had an element of genius about it. Matt had such flair. As a teenager, he was doing things with the ball that would make people go 'wow'. Al was not like that. He had determination and grit, he worked hard at his game and whether he was three yards or 30 yards from goal, Al would just leather it. The defender, the goalkeeper and the ball ended up in the back of the net if that was necessary.

He had that drive, that fire in his belly. He was fearless when he was attacking crosses and heading the ball, and that is what made him as a footballer. Every time a challenge was thrown down to him, he rose to it, starting with that hat-trick against Arsenal. I like to think this was the Southampton stamp, the attitude Dave Merrington demanded. These were Dave's standards.

I don't think anyone could have predicted that Al would go on to have quite such an incredible career but I was delighted for him as I saw him go from strength to strength. He was a big character, popular among his teammates and fun to be around. His confidence and personality grew alongside his progress as a player and that fuelled his ambition. It came at our cost on occasions, because he scored goals against us.

It was a strange dynamic when he first came back to face us with Blackburn, six months later. I knew him so well. We had always been close. My wife Karen and I often socialised with him and his wife, Lainya. And now it was my job to stop him. I tried to view him the same as any other opponent. There was no friendly interaction. We were both the same kind of personalities on the pitch. We knew what we had to do. I was in a Saints shirt, he was in a Blackburn shirt, we were opponents and not mates for 90 minutes.

Although it did feel different, at the end of a 1–1 draw, we shook hands and we wished each other well. There were further duels ahead. He will go down as one of the greats and I am pleased that Southampton was part of his journey, although naturally it would have been better if he could have stayed with us for just a little bit longer.

* * *

Personally, I never wanted to leave. I only ever wanted to play for Southampton. It was my city and my club. Although I realised I had to knuckle down if I was to cement my place in the team and play more games.

My approach was exactly as it had been in my teenage years. I was ultra-serious in the way I approached the game and I've always thought that was reflected in my style of play. It was different to other players.

I have never touched alcohol. I don't like the taste of beer and I have never been drunk. I didn't enjoy a lads' night out. That has never been a part of my life. It certainly went against the norm in those days. It is probably closer to the modern footballer. I can't think of another teammate who was teetotal. Most of the other players enjoyed a drink and the culture was firmly entrenched.

Even when there were parties and the guys were drinking, it only served to reinforce my feelings. I didn't want to drink. I didn't like it and I didn't like to see people drunk. I didn't want to be like that. That was how they wanted to relax and unwind. I was happier spending a night in front of the TV.

I was completely focused on my career. Having been brought up in a house where my mum and grandad both drank and smoked heavily, I knew that was certainly not going to help me achieve my ambitions.

Initially the players thought it was odd but it soon became, 'Oh, Franny doesn't drink' and they accepted that was how I was, part of my character. Some of them probably liked it because on the nights when I did go out with them I would be the taxi, picking them up and dropping them off at home. They were happy with the deal. I should have charged them a fare. It would have made up for my lack of goal bonuses.

I would join them once a week and I was out with some of the lads from the youth team when I met Karen in a bar. I was 19 and she was 18 and our relationship quickly became serious. On the night I first saw her I told the lads I would marry her one day. I didn't have the nerve to share that with Karen at the time but I felt like Bugs Bunny with cartoon love hearts coming out of his eyes. I knew I'd met someone special.

I broke into the first team about three weeks after we met, which she likes to take the credit for, and we settled down at an early age. Her family kindly embraced me and treated me like one of their own. I moved out of my mum's, which must have been quite tough for her, and in with Karen and her parents Bill and Eileen. They were such a close family and I loved it.

Bill was a long-standing Saints fan and had been a season-ticket holder from when I was a toddler. He was also a builder and built our first home for us, a four-bedroom detached house at the end of a private lane.

Karen became a big factor in the way I lived. Her love and support has been amazing in all aspects of my career. She has never wavered, always been on board with everything I have been passionate about. We married on 6 June, 1992 and continue to share the strongest and happiest friendship. She is my soulmate and I adore her. I love spending my time with her and she was at least a part of the reason why I was never too keen to go out with the lads.

My goal was to be a professional footballer at Southampton and I felt sure I needed to approach my career in this way if I was going to make it work. I was fiercely driven. Always feeling as if I was fighting for something. To earn my scholarship and then my first pro contract. To get into the team and then to stay in the team. To come out on top against an opponent in a game or against a teammate who was competing for my place. To convince another manager. To secure the next contract. To stay at the club I loved. To win the approval of the supporters. There was always something to fight for and I was always hungry to progress.

Sometimes I was fighting quite literally. Maybe it goes deeper into my background. I have always felt there was something for me to prove, especially in a football sense. All the way through my career I never felt comfortable. I never thought I had made it.

I suppose I've always wanted to please people: friends or family, supporters or management. We all like to be liked, don't we? When there were setbacks and the crowd was on my back or when I was dropped from the team, or was having a personal conflict in a game, the only thing I knew was to work harder and try harder.

From a young age, I had a vision of how I wanted my life to look. It sounds terribly cheesy, I know, but I pictured a family like the one I now have. I wanted to fall in love with a gorgeous woman, get married and live in a nice house with two children, a son and a daughter, be healthy and happy and enjoy life together.

My world was complete when Luke and Kenzie were born. I cried tears of joy, as well as tears of relief with Kenzie because her delivery was a little more traumatic. I was the happiest man alive. Luke was born in the summer of 1993 just five days before we were leaving on a preseason trip to Sweden. It was tough to leave both Karen and Luke behind. Kenzie was born almost two years later.

I have loved every second of being a dad. First words, first steps, first day at school, wonderful holidays, movie nights in at home. Karen and I are blessed with two amazing children who have grown into wonderful young adults and continue to make us overwhelmingly proud.

They graduated from university with firsts in their respective degrees and are thriving in their chosen professions. Luke's degree was in economics and he is enjoying a career as a private maths and economics tutor. Kenz studied multimedia journalism and is pursuing her childhood dream of being a presenter. She has carved out a fantastic career in children's television, and loves being on the mic every match day at St Mary's Stadium.

Coming from a broken background, I knew how I wanted to be as a husband and father. I did not have that perfect family when I was growing up. I had been adopted, then Mum and Dad split up when I was still only a baby. I saw Mum working hard and struggling. Maybe subconsciously I wished things had been different although, at the time, I didn't feel I was missing out on anything. I enjoyed my childhood.

Mum and I are complete polar opposites but I respect the way she is. She is a larger-than-life character. She loves to party and is a terrific cook. Her signature dish is a West Indian-style curry and we always try to persuade her to rustle one up when we visit.

Once, we were at her house when Karen suggested organising a family curry night and by the time we left, it had escalated into a huge Caribbean-themed party, with Mum drawing up a long list of names to be invited. Sure enough, a few weeks later, we all arrived in our fancy dress. There were some extravagant costumes on display and, as expected, everyone had an absolute ball. There have been no shortage of moments like this over the years and we have no end of hilarious and happy memories.

Mum had a long-term boyfriend called Leon Dalgetty who lived with us for many years when I was growing up. He was originally from Guyana and his easy-going nature was typical of his Caribbean roots. I spent a lot of time with Leon when I was young. I've always called him Chris because, for some reason, when I was little I thought his name was Chris, which makes it all very confusing. Karen likes to joke I am like Trigger always calling Rodney 'Dave' in Only Fools and Horses.

Leon was into his fitness and he gave me support even before I was serious about football. We would play badminton together at St Mary's sports hall. Later, when I was getting into football we'd be together at home and he'd get me to do some press-ups or sit-ups or go for a run, or we'd play table-tennis on the kitchen table, using books instead of a proper net.

He wasn't the biggest but he had a great physique. He worked out, did weights, he was strong and encouraged me to live a healthy lifestyle. He didn't smoke and he wasn't a drinker, although he did like to make me drink a concoction of Mackeson stout and condensed milk because he said it would bulk me up.

Fitness was his thing and it really rubbed off on me. Leon never had any doubt I could become a professional footballer. He had belief in me and that gave me confidence. He was a massive influence in many ways. I love him and have so many happy memories of the time I spent with him growing up.

He and Mum broke up when I was a teenager. We have kept in touch, for many years he was the father figure in my life. Much of the laid-back side of my character probably came from his influence.

Leon was a motor mechanic. He worked at a garage in Woolston on the river, across the water from St Mary's. There was a long service road, closed to the public, and it ran past the shipyards to a dead end. Before I was old enough to drive, he would say to me things like, 'Jump in that Mini and drive it up and down the road.'

He always had a few vehicles around. He would buy them, do them up and try to sell them on. I'd jump in and drive up and down. The first time he took me on public roads was when I was a learner driver. He climbed in beside me, reclined the passenger seat as far as it would go, closed his eyes and said, 'Off you go then.'

I passed my test first time and Leon did up a car for me: a Volkswagen Sirocco he put together from different parts and sprayed it silver. I was chuffed to bits with it. The boys in the youth team were getting their first cars and some of them were real beat-up bangers. I had this little resprayed VW flying machine.

One day I bumped into the back of another car. I wasn't going at any speed. I'd cracked his rear light but the front wing on my car had crumpled up and you could see all the filler inside it. The way it fell apart, it must have looked to the other driver as though I was in a clown's car.

Leon was friends with Gordon Greenidge, the legendary opening batsman for the all-conquering West Indies, who also played for 17 years for Hampshire. I think they met at the Northam Boys Club. He also knew John Holder, who played for Hampshire and went on to become an umpire. We'd spend time at Gordon's house and got the chance to know him. He would host barbecues and sometimes leave us tickets to watch Hampshire play at the old County Ground. In those days, there were plenty of vantage points. You didn't always need a ticket. I would sometimes clamber onto a wall to watch them play.

I once set the old VHS recorder to tape a televised game and ran down to the ground with a mate. We knew the camera angles and we climbed onto a wall and started to jump around and wave our arms. Then we rushed back home to check out the recording. Sure enough, there we were, larking around on national television.

I loved cricket at school and Gordon gave me a Gray-Nicolls bat with his signature stamped on it. I used it when I played cricket for the school team. This was my first recollection of being star-struck. The West Indies team was iconic at that time and dominated the sport for years, with dashing batsmen such as Viv Richards and Clive Lloyd, and their arsenal of quick bowlers. Malcolm Marshall and Andy Roberts, two of the most lethal fast bowlers of all time, played for a time at Hampshire. Gordon gave me a miniature bat signed by the entire squad, which I treasure to this day.

We took Gordon to the airport once when he was joining up with the squad to go on tour, and I went out to stay at his house in Barbados a couple of times, with Mum and Leon, and Karen. We were there once when Joel Garner popped in and he was an absolute giant, almost a foot taller than I was.

I continue to follow Hampshire closely. I will go to the Ageas Bowl to watch county cricket or an England game. Hampshire chairman Rod Bransgrove is a good friend and in recent years my attendance has become much more regular because Kenzie's fiancé, Lewis McManus, is in the first team, and we love to go along and cheer the boys on.

* * *

I may not have been at the heart of the Southampton dressing room social scene but I don't think anyone will ever say I wasn't a team player, or that I was less than 100 per cent committed to the group and its spirit.

I did miss some late-night antics because I was tucked-up in bed, and the lads would fill me in on the details the next day. There was one infamous occasion when a bonding exercise in Jersey descended into a scrap, with blows exchanged between David Speedie and Terry Hurlock in the hotel bar. A few words were traded and then Speedie threw a heavy glass ashtray towards Hurlock but, unfortunately, as it was flying through the air, Micky Adams leaned forward to pick up a drink and took the full force near one of his eyes, and that's when it all kicked off.

Sometimes, you could get the gist of what was going on without leaving your room. I was rooming with Matt Le Tissier on one trip into Europe when we were young. Matt wasn't much of a drinker either. He drank Malibu and Coke, which often prompted mickey-taking from the other lads, who were probably drinking something stronger. We were already back in our hotel room and we could hear Jimmy Case on the rampage in the corridors of the hotel.

Jimmy was worse for wear and he was prowling up and down, banging on all the doors. It sounded as if he was trying to get into the rooms. Matt and I were on our knees, peering through the crack under the door. We ignored Jimmy and pretended to be asleep until the storm passed. Next morning we set off to breakfast.

Andy Cook and Ray Wallace were rooming across the corridor from us and their door seemed to be open. Only, on closer inspection, the door was missing. Jimmy had knocked it clean off the hinges. We could see Andy and Ray in their beds, seemingly still in shock and it turned out all Jimmy was after was some fresh batteries for his Sony Walkman.

When you are inside the football bubble, these sort of things did not seem too far out of the ordinary. You have competitive individuals and a mix of characters, all thrown together – and they don't always like each other. Flash points might occur on the training ground, fuelled by competitive energy, or socially, fuelled by drink.

Sparks often flew during training sessions. It was almost a weekly occurrence. Someone would take offence to a challenge, something got said and, before you know it, you're pulling players apart.

I had my moments, most of them triggered by personal frustration, if I wasn't playing well or had been left out of the side. I have never understood why some managers would call a team meeting, name the team for the next day and then go out to train. If I was one of those not starting, I walked out of those meetings with my blood boiling. I'd rage at not being picked and go straight into training thinking about kicking somebody over the touchline. I'd fly into challenges and take people out.

Glenn Hoddle sometimes liked to do things that way. I always felt out in the cold when Glenn was in charge at Southampton and that came across in some of the flare-ups I had at the time. Some of my teammates felt the full force of my displeasure over his selection decisions. The only way to release my frustration was to let off steam and get aggressive.

There were occasions when I was out of order, whether that was with a teammate on the training ground or an opponent in a match. I would fly into someone with a strong challenge. Inside the club, people knew what I was like as a character and didn't really make an issue of it.

One clash with Ronnie Ekelund sticks in my mind. Ronnie was a young Dane, with us on loan from Barcelona and one of the nicest people on the planet. We signed him purely by chance, it seemed. We were on a preseason trip to the same place as Barcelona and our manager, Alan Ball, spent hours in company with their manager, Johan Cruyff. They had been world-class footballers and clearly enjoyed spending time together. And, at the end of the week, Bally came out of it with a new signing.

It seems crazy to think a major international transfer might unfold in this way, especially when you consider the level of forensic analysis that precedes a new signing in the modern Premier League.

Ronnie struck up a good understanding with Matt Le Tissier on the pitch. He was one of very few players ever on Matt's wavelength. He too had incredible skill and it probably wasn't a good thing to see me flaring up and having a go at him. We went in for a tackle and he made a little comment. Nothing nasty, he wasn't that sort of personality. But I snapped and I took out my anger on him. I pushed my forehead into his face, quite aggressively. There was no blood or breakages. It was over in an instant and I immediately felt bad about it. It was unfair of me to react the way I did and born purely out of the frustration of being dropped.

More commonly, sparks would fly when two edgy characters collided. I got into a scrape or two with Iain Dowie when we were teammates. We always got along perfectly well but he was a player who stood his ground and came back with a little bit. It is the nature of sport at this level. Players would not reach that level, or stay there, if they didn't have some of that competitive fire inside them.

It is not only down to talent. It was about wanting to win. Things would explode and then be forgotten almost as quickly. Once, it kicked off between Carlton Palmer and Robbie Slater. Punches were thrown. They went for it. Again, it was over in a few seconds. Another time, there was a bust-up one morning between Alan Shearer and Paul Rideout in the old gym at The Dell.

That place was a real gladiatorial environment, and the routine on a Friday was to train at the stadium. We warmed up on the track with some running and other exercises and then headed into the gym for a small-sided game, north v south or young v old. This was the day before a first-team fixture, and it seemed at times as if the managerial staff who refereed the games were intentionally trying to fire the lads up.

It was anything goes, no rules applied and the tackles went flying in. We were playing on hard wooden boards and any time the ball rolled into a corner you needed wing mirrors because someone would be coming in from behind to wipe you out.

Shearer and Rideout were running into a corner at the same time and Al shoulder-barged Paul when he wasn't braced for the impact. Paul went flying, smacked his head on the wall and his eye split open. There was blood everywhere and he was up, wanting to fight Al. This brought the session to an abrupt end.

I'm sure it was part of a deliberate plan by the staff to get our competitive juices flowing. They could see how it would escalate and they didn't stop it until it all boiled over, before blowing the whistle and saying, 'That's it lads, hit the showers, see you tomorrow.'

* * *

My aggressive style probably helped when Ian Branfoot came in to replace Chris Nicholl as manager. Chris was sacked in 1991 after six seasons in charge. We finished 14th in the league, a disappointment after finishing seventh the previous year. Ian didn't demand a lot of finesse and that didn't go against me. I played a fair bit during his time at the club.

The football can't have been great to watch. Chris's tenure had certainly been entertaining, with his liking for adventure and exciting young players coming through. In contrast, Ian's philosophy was to play very direct, not quite to Wimbledon levels, but we did play the percentages and went Route One, sticking the ball in the box. Some of our best players had been sold and Ian started to leave out Matt Le Tissier, who was our star.

That did not go down well with the fans. They idolised Matt and, when Ian dug his heels in, the animosity went up another level. The crowd turned on the manager. I felt for him, he was a decent guy. We worked with him day-to-day and I never had a falling out with him.

The same could not be said of a number of our supporters. They did not approve. It reached a point when the hatred towards him was hard to deal with. We'd be out on the pitch ready to kick off and you could feel the mood shift uneasily inside the stadium as soon as Ian appeared from the tunnel in the corner of the stadium and walked down the touchline to the dug-out.

Supporters are more than entitled to make their feelings known but it did nothing to help us keep our minds on the game when we were so aware of the depth of anger directed towards the manager. I had never experienced anything so negative at Southampton. It was really quite unpleasant and definitely a distraction.

We finished in the lower reaches of the league during Ian's two full seasons in charge, once flirting with relegation. In any of the cup competitions, though, we always felt as if we had a chance and, in 1992, we reached the FA Cup quarter finals.

Along the way, we won a memorable victory at Manchester United. We held them to a 0–0 draw at The Dell and were 2–1 up with seconds to go in the replay at Old Trafford when Brian McClair scored an untidy equaliser in stoppage time. Extra time was goalless and we went to penalties, only recently introduced to the FA Cup in order to cut down on the number of replays.

I was not among the nominated takers (no surprises there) and in truth had no desire to take one either. Matt Le Tissier fancied the glory of going last but didn't have the chance to take his penalty. United's Neil Webb blasted one over and Tim Flowers made the crucial save from Ryan Giggs to win it. Tim then showed an impressive turn of pace as he sprinted the length of the pitch towards our supporters. The adrenalin was pumping through his body and the rest of us were trailing behind him.

Progressing in the FA Cup was great but beating Manchester United was the real big thing. We rarely took a point from Old Trafford in the league. This was February 1992, the final season before the Premier League began. United were getting stronger, and they went on to win the title the following season with a team that would dominate English football for so many years.

Our bus was loaded up with alcohol for the long journey back to the south coast. We travelled everywhere by bus and often there would usually be drink involved on the way home, with the boys well and truly staggering around by the time we reached Southampton.

As for me, I'd climb on board and usually fall straight to sleep for the majority of the journey. Matt Le Tissier nicknamed me 'Bagpuss' after the sleepy cloth cat from the children's TV programme. It didn't go with my other nickname, which was 'Lean'. As in 'Lean Mean Fighting

Machine'. I think that one was Neil Ruddock's idea, based on my physique and fiery attitude on the pitch.

Matt once bought me a Bagpuss toy, which I still have in my house. Although when Bagpuss fell asleep on TV, so did all his friends. But when I fell asleep on the team coach, the lads on the back seats were more likely to be cracking open a beer or two and getting involved in a card school. This didn't bother me after a win. But if we'd lost, it would annoy me when some players came aboard the coach laughing and joking, behaving as if they'd forgotten about the game immediately.

After victory at Old Trafford, we scraped past Bolton in a fifth-round replay. Barry Horne scored from 40 yards in the last minute to take the tie into extra time, and his second of the night took us into the last eight of the competition.

I was starting to fancy our chances. Portsmouth were still in the competition and there was some excitement about the possibility of a derby. Instead, the draw pitched us at home against Norwich, who were struggling against relegation.

Once again, we drew the first tie 0–0 at The Dell and the semi-final draw was made before we met again for the replay. The winners would be going to Hillsborough to face Sunderland, then in Division Two, and we could see a route opening up to the final.

But we suffered from a disciplinary meltdown, on this occasion, nothing to do with me. A header from Neil Ruddock gave us the lead at Carrow Road but, early in the second half, Matt Le Tissier was provoked and sent off for a retaliatory kick at Robert Fleck. Norwich equalised and we held out to take the tie into extra time. We went down to nine men when Barry Horne became our second player sent off for aiming a kick at an opponent. Still, we clung on, resisting the pressure. Tim Flowers made some terrific saves and there were some frantic goal line scrambles.

We were five minutes from another penalty shootout when Chris Sutton claimed the winner and knocked us out. We were gutted. We knew we had blown a great chance. It made for a long and sombre journey home. Sunderland went and beat Norwich in the semi-final, before losing the final to Liverpool. This nagged away for many years as a big opportunity missed.

However, we did reach Wembley in 1992, in the final of a competition called the Full Members Cup, which was sponsored at the time by Zenith Data Systems, and also known as the ZDS Cup. It does not boast the prestige or glamour of the FA Cup but a crowd of nearly 68,000 showed what it meant to Saints and our opponents, Nottingham Forest, to be there.

It seemed like something for us to be proud of and, for me, it was nice to return to Wembley for the first time since the Schoolboy Internationals against Scotland and Netherlands. I was now there as a professional and that was evidence of my progress. Little did I know at the time I would never play there again.

For our supporters, it was a first trip to the stadium since the League Cup Final in 1979, a day when Saints lost 3–2 to Forest. Thirteen years on and, unfortunately, the result was identical. Forest were strong, with Brian Clough still in charge, and Stuart Pearce, Des Walker and Roy Keane in the team. Nigel Clough and Teddy Sheringham were up front. They beat us 3–2, with Scott Gemmill scoring twice, including the winner in extra time. Kingsley Black also struck. Our goals were scored by Matt Le Tissier and Kevin Moore.

Kevin, sadly, is no longer with us. He was a lovely guy, a centre-half who was brave and incredibly strong in the air, and his goal at Wembley that day was one of the best headers I ever witnessed.

Another vivid memory of him was after a match at The Dell. We had lost and Chris Nicholl picked up a milk bottle from beside the teapot and threw it down in anger. It was a general rant and not directed at anyone in particular. The bottle shattered on the floor in the centre of the dressing room. Milk and splinters of glass flew in all directions across the floor.

Chris carried on with his rant. He wasn't afraid to let people know when he wasn't happy but Kevin, stripped out of his kit and wearing only a towel around his waist, stood up and said, 'Oh, this is ridiculous.' He marched barefoot through the broken glass to the showers. The rest of us winced but Kevin did not break his stride and, fortunately, seemed to make it through unscathed.

He died in 2013, on his 55th birthday, far too young. He had been diagnosed with Pick's Disease, a rare form of dementia, in his late 40s. It did make me stop and think about the possible link between heading the ball and brain disease. There is more research and awareness around this now than there was at the time. I look back to how the centre-halves like Kevin would spend so much time heading the ball in training, not just in games. I headed plenty of footballs in training, and I know there were times when I put my head on the ball and saw stars, like a boxer taking a punch, and would need a few seconds to clear the brain fog.

If you asked me to pick an example of a player from my time at Southampton who was a master at heading the ball, I would say Kevin. He was dominant in the air. It is disturbing to think one of his great strengths as a footballer may have been a factor in his illness and tragic early death.

Research led by Dr Willie Stewart at the University of Glasgow and published in 2019 found that professional footballers were three-and-a-half times more likely to develop some form of dementia in later life than the general population. That is scary.

3

RED MIST

'There was a throw-in and I was standing on the touchline. I thought I was safe. Then I felt a knee at the base of my spine, on my coccyx. Franny caught me right on the bone. Two days later I could not move and a bruise had spread from the bottom of my back to my shoulder blades.

I came back to play against him when I was with Coventry, by which time I was 40 and knew I had to stay out of that radioactive zone. I was also the player-manager so I could say to myself it's best to keep away from him for tactical reasons.

On the pitch he never smiled, he just stared at you. I used to think there was something wrong with him. But, when I went there as manager, he was a real ally. He just wanted to do the right thing, and be a right good teammate.'

Gordon Strachan, Southampton manager 2001–04

Believe me, I am painfully aware of the perception many people formed of me when I was playing. To them I was a crazy thug on the pitch and I hated that.

Sent off again, I would feel instant regret and go through a period of remorse. I would sit in the dressing room, cut off and unable to help my team, thinking about what I would say to them. I would apologise to the players and the management. On one or two occasions, if it was appropriate, I'd say, 'Sorry guys but I felt hard done by, there.' My mind would turn a little bit to explaining myself to my wife Karen.

When I came home after a red card, and looked her in the eye, I would feel as though I had let everybody down. Not only Southampton FC and my teammates but my family and friends and, to a point, myself.

The last thing I wanted to do was to bring any shame on my family. I would go into Luke and Kenzie's rooms, stand at the end of their beds and apologise to them, even though they were sleeping and too young to understand. I knew they had to go to school and I would be wondering what the other parents were thinking.

I spent many hours brooding over the need to clean up my reputation. Karen and I had many conversations on the matter. She never read the riot act as such. I would know if she was angry and/or disappointed. One look was enough, and she would know when I was beating myself up.

She loved me and only saw me as her loving husband and a doting father. She knew it was my job. She knew what I was really like. Although, I must admit, there were times when I was concerned she might come along to a game, see this animal on the pitch and think again.

Southampton fans came to treat it all in good humour. Posters started to appear in doors and windows around the city, at one time, with a picture of my face on and the slogan: 'Beware! I live here.'

The Dell was such a tight and claustrophobic ground and as a player, when you were close to the touchline, the fans were easily within earshot and a particular section underneath the East Stand would sometimes join in a menacing stage whisper.

If the opposition winger came close or collected a ball which had rolled out of play and across the track they would sing quietly, 'Franny's gonna get ya.' That was always quite amusing. I remember David Beckham trotting by when he heard that and he looked straight at me. His expression said, 'Yeah, I know that's coming.'

Whenever I meet Saints' fans they seem to remember some of my wilder moments quite fondly. Those who supported other clubs, however, would have taken one look at the way I played and taken an instant dislike to me. They saw the red and yellow cards stacking up and it would only strengthen their opinion.

Just for the record, there were 11 red cards over my career at Southampton, and I realise that is quite an excessive number for the time when I played. Most of them were straight reds for flashes of anger or aggression. There were a few in the youth team and the reserves. There was one game in the reserves when we had three sent off in a 3–0 defeat at Norwich in January 1991. I was the first to go, sent off for a clash with Jeremy Goss in midfield. Initially, Goss was sent off and I was booked, but the linesman called the referee over to the touchline and whatever he said was enough to change my card from yellow to red.

Six minutes from time, Tommy Widdrington was the next to go, for an off-the-ball incident involving Chris Sutton, and Dean Radford quickly followed, sent off for something he said in protest to a linesman. My face must have been a picture when those two came in.

Another in the reserves came against Crystal Palace when they had a few big names in the team. Ian Wright and Mark Bright were playing and I was trying to fight my way through the ranks at the time. I was booked for a tangle on the touchline with Alan Pardew and sent off, half an hour later, for a second yellow for my reaction to a foul by John Pemberton. The match report in the *Southern Daily Echo* said the referee had given me several warnings and was left with no choice. I was quoted too, promising to calm down and keep my head but it would take me a while.

I certainly did not set out to be some kind of hard-man figure. I had played with genuinely tough players, such as Jimmy Case and Terry Hurlock, and I would not dream of putting myself in the same bracket. Jimmy was the minder for all the young Saints players when we were coming through. If someone tried to bully us during a game, he would move in and sort it out. Perhaps, in my later years, I tried to protect some of the young players in a similar way but I have never considered myself to be in the 'tough guy' category.

What I had was a great will and desire to win, and my natural aggression was a key part of my weaponry. I wanted to dominate my opponent. I knew my strengths as a footballer and wanted to use them to help my team. I am quite certain I would not have been the same player and would not have enjoyed the same career if my attitude had been any different.

It was the tackle on John Fashanu at Plough Lane in March 1990 that seemed to earn me a degree of notoriety. It wasn't triggered by anything more than my sheer determination not to be intimidated by a formidable Wimbledon team who revelled in their Crazy Gang reputation.

Fashanu was a big, strong striker who was nicknamed Fash the Bash by the media. He would stand in the corridor as the away teams arrived, posturing and eye-balling you, with his muscles oiled up. These were the mind games of the time. It was a hostile welcome at Wimbledon, designed to warn you of the physical encounter you knew you were going to have on the pitch. This is going to hurt, are you ready for the battle? They had some aggressive players: Fash, Vinnie Jones and Dennis Wise, who had started out at Southampton.

I was a young defender, 21 years old at the time, not long since broken into the first team and I wanted to stand up to that. Maybe I took it a step too far on that occasion. Fashanu had just scored and we were losing 3–1. I went into the challenge thinking there was a chance to take the ball and leave a bit on him. He just got there ahead of me, then somersaulted over me and landed in a heap, making it seem spectacular. Matt Le Tissier tried to persuade the referee he was making a meal of it but I got my marching orders.

It was caught on camera and shown on television, which not everything was in those days, and has proved to be quite popular with Southampton fans over the years, judging by the amount of times it surfaces in conversation and the number of times the clip has been viewed on YouTube.

This was the first red card of my senior career and, although it might have helped me find a way into the affections of some Saints supporters, it did unwittingly set me down a path towards earning an unwanted reputation.

A few years and a couple of red cards later, Sir Alex Ferguson had a go at me in the newspapers after I had clashed with Andy Cole during the second half of a 4–1 defeat at Manchester United. I wouldn't describe it as a fully blown head butt but it was true that I did put my head into his face and somehow managed to come out of it worse, with a cut on my head where I bumped into Andy's teeth. The blood poured from the wound and made for quite an alarming photograph. One or two United fans stayed behind after the match to yell abuse at me as we climbed onto the team bus outside Old Trafford.

I wasn't sent off on that occasion – maybe I should have been – but the comments from Sir Alex turned it into a big story. *The Sun* printed the photo of me with my face covered in blood under the headline 'Bloody Nutter' and one of their reporters called me at home looking for a comment. All the criticism caused me more pain than the cut on my head.

Years later, when I was celebrating my 40th birthday, we invited some friends over for dinner and a few drinks. Karen had a selection of photographs blown up and laminated and stuck them around the house as a surprise when I came downstairs. Among all the happy family photos was a photocopy of the 'Bloody Nutter' headline and image from the game against Manchester United. It was something I'm really not proud of. In my mind it just wasn't me, at least not in the setting of the family home.

That was me in a working environment, where there was almost an element of acting involved, where I adopted a persona, put on a front or exaggerated part of my personality for effect to let opponents know

I wouldn't be messing about today. I have never been able to shake from my mind a remark once made to Karen by someone who was offering her sympathy because they thought it must be terrible being married to somebody like me. They were insinuating that it must have been like living with a monster. Wow, that was a low point.

Until then, I'd given very little thought to the idea that anyone might form an opinion of my suitability as a husband or father simply by watching a game or reading the paper, or hearing somebody talk about me. That wasn't a particularly nice thing to consider.

* * *

Other problems emerged from the red mist moments. One of them was the financial impact. One sending off was a fine of half a week's wages. If it happened a second time in the same season it was one week's wages. If it happened a third time it was two weeks' wages.

Then you were banned and therefore lost out on appearance money and any win bonuses, which made a big difference to your pay packet. I wasn't on a huge salary. And, of course, you lost your place in the team and might not get it back any time soon if your replacement was playing well.

Losing my place also meant extra physical work in training to keep my fitness levels up. I just wanted to be out there playing. There was always a deep sense of disappointment when I was unable to play or left out and there would inevitably be stories in the newspapers, claiming Saints were losing patience and trying to sell me.

In the 1996–97 season, I picked up three red cards in just a few months, one of them while playing in the reserves, again at Norwich. The *Echo* described it as a 'retaliatory lunge', 35 seconds into the second half. The referee was Paul Vosper, the same referee who sent me off playing for the reserves in the Combination at Norwich in 1991. I missed 13 matches because of suspension over the course of that campaign.

It certainly made a dent in my earnings and we had a mortgage to pay. I had to meet with Brian Truscott, the club secretary, and ask him if I could organise a standing order to spread out the cost of my repayments.

There was an occasion when I was hauled before an FA disciplinary panel. I reported to the FA headquarters, then at Lancaster Gate, in London, with Keith Wiseman, one of the Southampton directors, and I thought we were going for a bit of a chat. I could not believe how many people were sitting on the panel. They tore into my history of misdemeanours, reading out my record of red and yellow cards before I had any chance to put my case across.

I was on the back foot. I went in there thinking I didn't deserve to be sent off for the incident and I had no idea what to say to defend myself against this barrage of accusations. The ban was upheld, perhaps unsurprisingly, and I was fined. More expense.

* * *

There's always been fire in my belly and over the years there were several attempts by various managers to bring it under control using different techniques, ranging from the dressing room tirade to a quiet word in my ear.

Chris Nicholl was the first to address it in the early days with the change of position from striker to midfield, and then to left-back. This was a conscious decision to move my position to help me control my disciplinary problems. Chris was worried I might end up with a reputation. Ultimately I did, so I guess he failed on that score, but not for want of trying.

My first sending off was in a youth team League Cup final against Crystal Palace. We were playing at The Dell in the days when I was still a striker. I scored a goal and we won but I got myself into a tangle with their goalkeeper. I thought he had hold of my leg and I lashed out with my boot in an attempt to get him off me and caught him in the face. It was a straight red.

Dave Merrington, our youth team coach at the time, was normally prepared to back me. He liked my aggression and commitment. This was a night, however, when he tore a strip off me, big time. He went to town, making clear this type of reaction was not acceptable. This was a big game and it could have cost us. I was shaking in my boots.

I didn't get into many scrapes when I was younger. I was big and always ready to look after myself and maybe the other kids took one look at me and thought they would rather not take me on, they kept their distance.

As I moved into the professional game, I found a lot more like-minded people, driven to win and be successful. I felt as though I needed to be on this footing whenever I pulled on my boots to play, even in training sessions. I felt like I was fighting for everything. Not only was I competing to win the ball in a tackle or to win a game with my team but I was fighting my own corner. I was fighting to keep my job and to earn my living.

In my head, this was a day-to-day thing. I was never in a position where I was comfortable enough to relax and take things easy. I was intense. I had an extreme determination and I had to perform at this level all the time. I had to be at full throttle, and on the pitch the aggression came out.

I relished the physicality of the contest. I enjoyed engaging in a battle. I know that might sound weird. I loved to come off the pitch exhausted, when I knew I had engaged physically and we had kept a clean sheet, and won the game. I would get a tremendous buzz from that.

Rarely did I go in for any verbal intimidation. My focus was fiercely trained on doing my own thing. However, there were times when I might have a passing word in an opponent's ear to mention in the nicest possible way that it was going to be a tough day for them.

I was very serious about my football. In fact, I was obsessive. Maybe that's why I lived my life the way I did. I wanted to give myself every chance to be the best I could be at three o'clock on a Saturday.

For years, I stuck to a mechanical routine. On a match day, I always put on my left sock first and my left boot. I tapped the post of the handrail at the top of the staircase leading down from the dressing rooms at The Dell. I tapped the post at the top and the bottom.

I ate beans on toast as my pre-match meal without fail until I was into my 30s, but when Glenn Hoddle came to the club as manager, he told me beans did not give me the requisite energy to sustain me for 90 minutes. I thought, 'Blimey, I've been doing this for years, why should I change?' But I did change, to pasta, because he convinced me it was better and I wanted to do it right.

* * *

When it came to routines and superstitions there was no one quite like John Burridge, who was our goalkeeper at Southampton for two years from 1987, around the time when I was breaking into the team. Known to all as Budgie, he was one of the great characters of that era. He was something of a veteran when he joined us at the age of 35, and he was still playing in non-league 10 years later.

Chris Nicholl signed him when Peter Shilton left for Derby. Budgie liked to hype himself up, always talking to himself and telling anyone who wanted to listen that he was England's number one and not Shilts. He would sign his autographs as 'England's Number 1' and had a speedball punchbag, which he used for boxing work. He drew a face with 'SHILTS' written on it and gave it a smack as he walked past.

Budgie liked to listen to motivational messages on a tape. He'd take himself off somewhere quiet to lie down, stick on his headphones and listen to them on an old cassette player. He would make some strange facial expressions as he listened intently, muttering to himself, 'Budgie, you are England's number one' and 'Budgie, you are the greatest goalkeeper.'

That was his pre-match routine and we had no idea how sacred it was until one day when Matt Le Tissier interrupted it. Matt wanted him to sign a programme or a ball so he went up to him and tapped him on the shoulder. Budgie was immersed in his tape, deep in mindfulness and completely flipped at the intrusion. Matt was petrified as Budgie went after him.

Budgie also had some strange kit choices, including a tight-fitting garment that I think was a woman's girdle. He would strap himself in, taking particular care to tuck away the most delicate parts of the male anatomy before pulling on his shorts. When we asked him what he was doing, he explained that he tucked it all out of the way so that he could spread his legs to block a shot and know there was nothing dangling in the line of fire.

In the team hotel, in order to sharpen up his reaction times and test his reflexes, he would say to his roommates, 'See that bowl of fruit? At any point without warning, I want you to throw that orange at me.'

In the shooting sessions, he would fly into a rage if others were not at the same level of intensity. When one of the young lads jogged casually into a shot and smashed the ball past him, he exploded. 'Too slow,' he was shouting. 'Too slow, two seconds, two seconds, like in a game, too slow.' He didn't like the way the lad ambled into the shot because it wasn't realistic.

He made us laugh. We were on our way to a reserve game in London and he was regaling us on the bus with stories about his tough upbringing in Cumbria. We were driving through one of the rougher areas of the capital and Budgie was looking out of the window.

'This takes me back boys,' he was saying. 'We didn't have much when I was a lad. We didn't have much money, there was no money for a school uniform, my mum would send us down to the Army and

Navy stores to kit us out.' Then he paused for effect and added, 'Boys, it was no fun going to school dressed as a Japanese general, I can tell you.'

* * *

I was nowhere near Budgie's levels of obsession but I did try to prepare for every game with the same routine and careful attention to detail. By the time kick-off came around, I had worked myself into a state where I would be pacing about and visualising the first tackle, my first chance to put in a hefty challenge.

There were occasions when I flew in, thinking there was a chance to catch the opposition player. And there were times when I knew I had caught someone and had the desired effect. I'd be lying to say otherwise. I figured I had to do it, either to gain an advantage on my opponent or take them out of the game to a degree. At the very least, I wanted to make them think about the next challenge and put them in two minds about what they wanted to focus on.

We didn't have all the modern analysis equipment but we learned about the strengths and weaknesses of our opponents. Sometimes I had specific man-marking duties. It was my job to nullify others.

I came to the position late but I became a decent defender. I was quick and able to get around the pitch. I was tenacious, good in the air for my size and I could run. My fitness levels were always high and I soon came to appreciate that defending was what I was best at.

When I encountered a young Roy Keane playing wide on the right for Nottingham Forest, I thought it might be a good idea to put down a marker on him with a strong challenge early in the game. Sometimes if you did that to a young winger they would disappear. You hit them hard and looked in their eyes and you could tell if they were up for the scrap or not.

I snapped into a tackle on Keane, and thought, 'Right, that's him sorted.' Five minutes later, I got the ball and he came crashing through the back of me. It was a similar challenge to mine but with interest added. This was not someone who was easily intimidated. I went on to play against him on many more occasions when he was at Manchester United, by which time he had switched into central midfield, which meant I did not come up directly against him much – and maybe that was not a bad thing.

* * *

There was no shortage of big, strong centre-forwards. Fashanu was at Wimbledon and Mick Harford played for several clubs during that era including Luton and Derby. They were players who had presence and liked to let you know they were there. Martin Allen, playing for West Ham at the time, caught me with an elbow above one of my eyes and left me needing stitches. There were others, such as Alan Shearer and Mark Hughes, who were tough, both mentally and physically, and not afraid to mix it. Some wanted to go to war. Some wanted to stay out of your way, which was perfect, job done.

Others would get verbal, like Ian Wright. I always found Wrighty difficult to handle. He was an incredible goalscorer with speed, fabulous movement and a fiery side to his nature, and he could stand up to any physical intimidation. Verbally he was a pain in the neck and did not miss a chance to have a go at you, and if you made a comment he came straight back.

Others preferred to quietly carry on and let their football do the talking. Dennis Bergkamp was like that. There was a game against Arsenal when I was playing at centre-half with Ken Monkou, against him and Wrighty. Bergkamp was playing well and had scored a brilliant goal to put them 2–1 up. I said to Ken, 'Come on, time to go to town on these two, let's step it up.'

When the chance came, I stepped on Bergkamp's foot. I could tell I'd hurt him. I wanted to disrupt his thought process. I wanted to give him something to think about besides what he was doing with the ball. Quite naturally, he didn't take too kindly to this but he didn't swear and he didn't react. He didn't jump up and push me. He didn't go looking for physical revenge. Soon afterwards, another ball was played into him. My eyes lit up again. I fancied another piece of him. I went careering in but he knew what was going on. He must have been still silently raging from the previous incident. He stepped into me with his shoulder and sent me flying. Then he dribbled into the penalty box and smashed the ball into the back of the net, 3–1. The perfect response. Oh great, I thought.

Wrighty was unable to contain himself. He knew what had been going on and was sure to make the most of this, enthusiastically celebrating the goal right in front of me. He yelled, 'Thanks Franny, I've never seen him so fired up'. He couldn't stop laughing or rubbing it in whenever he was near me or ran by me.

There had been a time when I didn't like Wrighty on the pitch. Not only was he an incredibly tough opponent, I thought he came across as arrogant when he was playing, but my view of him changed after a game against Arsenal. I was in the players' lounge with my son Luke, who was still very young at the time, and in my arms. Wrighty came over and smiled, and he asked, 'Is this little Franny?' We started talking and it soon became clear to me what a lovely guy he was, completely different to his personality on the pitch. If I couldn't understand that, then who could?

I invited him to play in my Testimonial. He couldn't play but sent me a signed copy of his book to raise some funds. Soon after, we were in opposition again at The Dell and I got him booked. The referee gave a foul against Wrighty and he didn't retreat quickly so I kicked the ball at him on purpose. 'Thanks for that, Franny,' he fumed. 'I sent you that book down and you go and do that… this place is s***, the ground's s***, the team is s*** and you're s***'. Normal service had been resumed.

* * *

Graeme Souness once told me, during his time in charge at Southampton, that if he was playing against me, the first thing he would do would be to stamp on my foot. I had been looking forward to working with Souness. He was an exceptional player with a very tough streak to his game. He also had a fierce reputation as a manager, although it is fair to say he had mellowed a bit by the time he joined Saints.

We never sat down to have an in-depth conversation about my disciplinary record but this aside on the training pitch might have been his way of passing on his advice. He thought if he stamped on my foot, he could provoke a reaction and that would have a negative impact on my performance. There were certainly times when I should have been smart enough to control my emotions, and I am sure some players set out to wind me up intentionally.

Equally, there were times when my temper snapped without the slightest provocation. I could be my own worst enemy. The red mist would descend. Teammates started to see the signs and they would walk by and tell me to 'relax' or 'be careful'. Matt Le Tissier, as a close friend, tried reasoning with me but there were times when I was beyond listening. It is a weird place to be. My switch was flicked and even if I could hear the words of advice I could not click out of that angry mode.

When I was sent off, the red mist would disperse equally quickly and I would be left thinking 'oh no'. I would have put my team under pressure in the match, whatever the situation might have been.

There were times when my reaction was well out of proportion. Sometimes I would be kicking off at something as daft as a referee's decision. My lights would go on, the eyes would roll a little bit and I would be raging beyond reason. The match officials were not always at the top of my Christmas card list. They will insist there is no bias and those I have met since I retired naturally all tell me the same thing. But if you're a club the size of Southampton and you're playing at Anfield or Old Trafford you do feel the decisions go against you.

I'm not saying the officials were corrupt but I would say they were easily swayed, sometimes by the intensity of the home crowd, sometimes by the manager if it was someone like Sir Alex Ferguson, sometimes by any big-name players on parade. Little things, like fouls and free-kicks went against us because we were 'just Southampton'.

We have all tried to referee the game at times, to get in the ref's ear and say little things to make them realise what's going on. 'Come on ref, you're not going to let him get away with that are you?'

And there were times in the dressing room when we would say it was time to get around the officials and put them under some pressure. I was an apprentice when I heard Mark Dennis saying, 'Right lads, anything kicks off, every single one of us pile in, the ref can't send us all off.'

That was Mark's mentality. He was a fabulous footballer who left us for QPR before I broke into the first team. There was an explosive side to his character, similar to myself, and he sometimes fell on the wrong side of the officials.

The referees I liked were those who engaged with you and might have a chat in the tunnel or even during the game and build a rapport. Dermot Gallagher was like that. I never had any problems with him. Others I clashed with, like Graham Poll. For whatever reason we took an instant dislike to each other and he sent me off three times during my career.

One of those was for what he adjudged to be an elbow aimed at Ruel Fox at the Milton Road end of The Dell, about an hour into a 1–0 defeat against Norwich on New Year's Day in 1994. That one was particularly harsh, and a strange decision as the free-kick was given in our favour.

Southampton studied the video and lodged an appeal. The incident happened at a time when the FA were trying to clamp down on the use of the elbow because Fashanu had shattered Gary Mabbutt's cheekbone a few weeks earlier during a game between Wimbledon and Tottenham. My appeal was rejected and I served a three-match ban.

I was also sent off for an elbow on Dean Sturridge against Derby in May 1998. He was pulling at my shirt and I was trying to shake him off. I can argue all day long about that one, which isn't always the case.

The one at Bolton, five months earlier, involved me giving Jamie Pollock a tap round the face. It was a silly thing to do. I know you can't raise your hands and touch an opponent. The game had stopped, there had been a few words exchanged and I tapped him around the face as I turned to jog off.

He didn't make a meal of it, to be fair to him. The referee, Gary Willard, just happened to be right there on the spot and he pulled out the red card. Rightly so, I guess. Worse still, it was in the first half, which meant my teammates had to play for almost an hour with 10 men. They did well to leave with a 0–0 draw.

Another of the Graham Poll dismissals was an off-the-ball clash with Trevor Morley in an FA Cup tie against Reading at Elm Park. It was January 1997, the pitch was frozen, rock-hard and clearly not fit to play. When we arrived and took a look at the pitch, I don't think any of us expected to play. When we found out the game was on, we thought it was a joke. Maybe we weren't in the right mind-set. We were 2–1 down when I caught Trevor Morley with an elbow. Dave Beasant was coming out to collect a ball and I was trying to block Morley's run. I should have been smarter about it but that's what I was like at the time, playing with a lot of anger. I wanted to do well and win but obviously I stepped outside the laws of the game on a number of occasions.

Not only did I leave my team with 10 men but my foul conceded a penalty and Morley scored Reading's third from the penalty spot. We lost 3–1 and were out in the third round, beaten by a team struggling in the bottom half of the second tier, then known as Division One before it had been rebranded as the Championship.

Robbie Slater was sent off in the closing seconds of the same game at Reading for something he had said to one of the linesmen, and we finished the match with nine men. Then Graeme Souness landed himself in trouble for confronting Poll on the pitch after the final whistle. It was a bad day all round.

You could see the way one or two referees took pleasure as they issued cards, or the way they spoke down to you. I was coming on as a substitute at West Ham in August 1996 when the linesman made a clever comment along the lines of, 'Don't go doing anything silly today.' I was thinking, 'Hang on, I'm only just coming on.' Maybe he had seen the script. I had only been on the pitch for 26 minutes when I lost the plot and referee David Elleray sent me off for quite a hefty tackle on Paolo Futre. Frustration was building up in the game and I wasn't playing particularly well. I'll always maintain it wasn't malicious. It looked worse than it was because he ended up on the running track. I stepped over him as he was rolling about.

At Tottenham, in February 1993, I was sent off as we somehow conceded four goals in five minutes at the start of the second half. From being 1–0 up at half time, we were suddenly 4–1 down with an hour gone. My response was to go flying into a challenge on Nicky Barmby. I was high and he ducked. I didn't catch him as such but off I went.

I was in the bath when Kerry Dixon came in for a shower. I think his chance of getting on as a substitute had disappeared in the tactical changes we had to make to cover up for my dismissal. Kerry said, 'It's not good Franny, you're not forging the best of reputations for yourself but in the future this might help you.'

It was an interesting view from a teammate. I hadn't done him any favours with my antics. I hadn't helped my team. He was trying to be supportive by saying it may make opponents a little more wary when playing against me. Teammates at least were able to see both sides of me. They usually saw the mild mannered me. Off the pitch, I can raise my voice in an argument but I have never had cause to explode in the same way or get physical as I would on the pitch.

Nor have I encountered any post-match problems with opponents who were out in search of retribution. The way I played it's quite easy to imagine me coming out of the dressing room at Plough Lane to find Fash standing there waiting for me. Maybe once the intensity of the game had worn off, they realised there was no nastiness involved.

A lot of the challenges perceived as bad ones over the years might have been a little bit late but they were genuine attempts to win the ball.

When I watch modern football, it seems the defenders are more interested in looking good on the ball, going off on a little dribble perhaps or spraying passes around, than they are about getting stuck into the defensive aspect of the game, winning the ball and protecting their goal.

Technically, football has become much better but an important element has been lost by reducing the physical nature of the game, and that has been detrimental to the spectacle.

I experienced the very beginnings of the trend towards gamesmanship, with players trying to con referees by diving around to win free-kicks and penalties, or trying to prompt red and yellow cards for opponents. That infuriated me. I came from an era where most players, if they were hit, would do everything in their power not to show they were hurting.

When I started to see players falling over having barely been touched or, on some occasions, not touched at all, it made my blood boil. It would have given me more of a reason to want to kick them. It is just as well I played when I did, but I would point out that I did make it through the last five years of my career without a red card. And the last two reds were very soft: the tap on Pollock at Bolton and the harsh decision by Mike Riley to send me off for an elbow against Derby.

My disciplinary record did improve. There was no single moment when the clouds parted and everything changed, it was more of a gradual process. There were several things at play and I was maturing as a person and as a footballer.

I had grown up as a striker with others trying to stop me. When I first became a defender, I wanted to win every ball. It took time for me to learn that was not possible. Nor was it necessary. You can defend well without having to win the ball. I learned to control my aggression more efficiently and I became a little less rash. I became a better player when I understood I did not have to tear into every challenge and take a piece of the opponent.

Maybe some of the advice from Dave Merrington, Chris Nicholl, Graeme Souness and Kerry Dixon seeped through eventually. Maybe Kerry was right, with a reputation forged, the silent threat was enough to subdue those players who might be put off their game by such things, and it saved me the need to physically go through with it.

I had won over the majority of the Southampton supporters, too, which was always important to me. I have come to know so many fans personally over the years, from encounters outside the stadium on match days, and they are a huge reason the club is so special. Often, they have been going to games since I was playing and are still there, and have supported Southampton through thick and thin for many years.

Some of them gave me stick when I first broke into the team and my passing wasn't perfect but they came to understand me. I felt less of an urge to prove to them how committed I was. These factors all played a part and I became a little less volatile on the pitch. Although, I'm not sure if anyone ever noticed.

4

SURVIVAL INSTINCT

'Franny is my sort of man, a solid character with a true desire to win. Aggressive, sometimes over-aggressive, which I quite liked, and when he went out on the pitch you knew, as a manager, that he was giving you everything. You knew the person up against him would not enjoy the experience.

Off the pitch he offered an opinion but he didn't complain, he was onside with what you were trying to do and he would always look in the mirror before pointing a finger at anyone else. That's unusual.

When things go wrong in a dressing room, people look around and start to blame each other. We had a limited squad during my season at Southampton and we escaped relegation by the skin of our teeth. From start to finish, it was a battle and Franny's attitude was just to get on with it. He was one of those players you wanted with you in the trenches.'

Graeme Souness, Southampton manager 1996–97

There's only one way to play. You play to win and I would love to reflect on my football career and write about the silverware we collected at Southampton. That wasn't quite how it worked out, unfortunately, but I am still very proud of the fact that in all my time at the club we were never relegated from the top flight.

With the resources we had, playing at The Dell, where the capacity became smaller as the all-seater stadium regulations were enforced, and with the resources we were up against as the Premier League was established and the biggest clubs became bigger and richer, that is a huge sense of achievement.

Every year we were written off. Sometimes written off before a ball had been kicked and every year we used that as a source of motivation to drive the group. We came to relish proving people wrong. Some years we came closer than others to the drop but we always found a way to survive. The Saints became the masters of the relegation escape and the more times we escaped the more confident we became.

We almost slipped into trouble in 1992–93, Ian Branfoot's second season as manager and the inaugural season of the Premier League. We had sold some promising players, including Alan Shearer and Neil Ruddock, and suffered a late slump in form, losing six of our last eight games. We crashed from a reasonably healthy position in the top half to finish in 18th, taking only one point from the last four games. It was my fifth season involved with the first team and my first real close shave with relegation. By the end, we were only a point clear of the drop zone at a time when there were 22 teams in the division and three went down but we knew we were safe before the final day. Fortunately, we had collected enough points during a good spell of seven wins in 11 games between mid-January and mid-March.

Twelve months later and we were much deeper in the mire, stranded inside the bottom three for the first half of the season. In January, Lawrie McMenemy returned to the club as director of football, and not long afterwards Ian Branfoot was dismissed as manager and replaced by Alan Ball.

Bally oozed football. He was a former Saints player under Lawrie, so he knew the club and what it stood for and he had a rapport with the supporters, commanding instant respect as part of the England team that won the World Cup in 1966.

Though not the biggest in terms of size he brimmed with energy and charisma and was a real positive force. His passion for the game rubbed off on everybody. He could get upset at times. There were five-a-side games when he joined in and if his team was getting thumped then he would just pick up the ball and walk off the pitch. He was a winner, he did not like to lose, not even in a five-a-side, and the players adored him.

There were days he came in and said, 'Right lads, one hour of quality and then you can go home.' We'd look at each other thinking, 'Come on, do this right and we're out of here by 11.30 a.m.' And, if we performed well, he was good to his word. If he got the standards and the intensity he was looking for we would finish early. If he didn't, we'd stay out until he did and we always knew when he was angry because he would tear off his flat cap and throw it on the floor, whether that was in the middle of a training session or a match.

Both he and Lawrie recognised that Matt Le Tissier was our star and the rest of the players were happy with that. No one in the dressing room thought differently. We didn't have any egos.

Matt visibly grew in stature when Bally made it crystal clear he was our main asset. He made him captain and gave a speech to the squad about Matt. He said he was the best player in England and one of the best in Europe, and it was our job to get the ball to him. Personally, I thought that was great. Win the ball and give it to Matt; that was more or less what I tried to do anyway.

In the same way Bally got the best out of Matt, he helped me grow as a player. When he and Lawrie made Matt the team captain they felt it would be a good idea to share his workload and asked me to take on the role as club captain. It was such an honour to be considered one of the senior voices in the dressing room and represent the club in the community. I was 25 at the time and had been around the first team for a few years.

I held the position as club captain for the rest of my playing career at Saints, regardless of whether I was in or out of the team. Bally also trusted me with more responsibility on the pitch. Rather than worry about my limitations, he focused on my qualities as a defender – I could make things difficult for my opponents.

Bally understood me, and he got the best out of me. He told me I was good at what I did and important for the team. He was the first manager to detail me as a man-to-man marker, and sometimes played me as a centre-half with instructions to track one particular opponent around the pitch, effectively taking them out of the game.

Naturally, this would be their star man. I was deployed to put the shackles on players like Eric Cantona, Jurgen Klinsmann, Alan Shearer, Ian Wright and Dennis Bergkamp. These were some of the finest strikers in the world and it was my job to keep them quiet. Or try to. It didn't always work, I will be the first to admit, but I did enjoy the challenge and I feel I always did a good job in that role.

When I am at speaking engagements or at fans' events people always want to know about my toughest opponents. They were all tough in some shape or form. Klinsmann, at Tottenham, had lightning pace and read the game exceptionally well. His movement was extraordinary. He drifted on your shoulder, making it difficult to keep him in your field of vision, and you knew what a goal threat he was.

Cantona had genuine presence. His confident swagger, bordering on arrogance, typified Manchester United at the time. United knew they were a great team, they knew they had great players and he was their talisman. He had an aura. He lined up next to you in the tunnel with his collar turned up and his barrel chest puffed out, eyes straight ahead as if he could not wait to get the game started. With the ball at his feet he could do incredible things and he didn't always have to be running around to exert his influence on the game. They looked to him in the way we looked to Matt Le Tissier.

At 5ft 9ins, I was not the tallest of defenders and I learned techniques to combat bigger and stronger opponents. I would stick my hip into them to knock them slightly off balance in a certain situation. Tackling fast and hard was part of my armoury but, increasingly, we were coming up against players on another level. Gianfranco Zola had such an influence when he joined Chelsea and, for all his individual brilliance, he left me with the feeling he was one of the least selfish opponents I came up against, who took as much pleasure from creating a goal for a teammate as he did scoring himself.

* * *

My first appearance under Alan Ball was in his first home game as Southampton boss. It was Valentine's Day 1994 at The Dell against Liverpool, live on Sky Sports, and there were snow flurries during the game. I was just back from suspension, after the Ruel Fox red card.

We won 4–2 in a brilliant game – another Le Tissier hat-trick – and our form picked up. We won the next game 1–0 at home to Wimbledon – Le Tissier again. We climbed to 17th, but we were unable to pull clear of danger and became ensnared in a real fight for survival.

Any relegation fight over the years came to consume my every waking thought. I would put my head on the pillow at night thinking about the position we were in and the importance of staying up and the repercussions it would have on a club like Southampton if we went down. In those times, I could not shake it from my mind. The pressure builds and it takes a lot to hold your nerve and to keep the belief. I would settle into a blinkered mind set, one where you train, play, get the result and move onto the next fixture. We became familiar with the routine over the years and that experience helped us.

Another key factor was our spirit. Southampton remained a family club long after other clubs had turned into slick business operations and that helped us through some of these desperate situations. We did feel like a family. Everyone was in it together, and it has remained that way. Many of the backroom staff and stewards who were working at Southampton during my playing days are still at the club and, even after all this time, there is a real warmth and sense of familiarity when I am at St Mary's.

Football was changing fast in the '90s but long-serving directors and staff members, and a core of players who had come up through the ranks or had been with us for many years meant our bonds were still tight.

We didn't have the best financial resources so we had to rely on spirit and togetherness, and the supporters played a huge part in keeping us in the Premier League over the years. There was always a connection between them and the team and it always gave us strength. And it helped, of course, to have a player like Matt Le Tissier.

The outlook was particularly bleak as the 1993–94 season reached the closing stages. Despite the initial bounce after Alan Ball replaced Ian Branfoot, we lost three games in a row around Easter – against Oldham, Chelsea and Manchester City – and were back into the bottom three when we went to Norwich on 9 April. At Carrow Road, with less than an hour gone, we were 3–1 down. We looked doomed. Then Matt sprang into action, scoring another hat-trick to get us back in the game.

So we were level at 4–4 with seconds to go when Matt delivered the corner from which Ken Monkou headed in the winning goal. What a comeback that was. We all sprinted across to the travelling Saints fans. Ken threw the ball in with them, on the understanding that it would not come back quickly. This was long before anyone came up with the multi-ball system. I'm sure we would not have escaped relegation without turning that game around and winning at Norwich.

Morale was lifted by the nature of the victory and we followed it up with good wins against Aston Villa and Blackburn. There were setbacks as we lost at Tottenham and Manchester United but we went to West Ham on the final day of the season confident we could get the result we needed. A win and we were definitely safe. A draw might be enough. Swindon were definitely down and only the most freakish sequence of results could save Oldham. The third and final relegation place would go to one of four clubs: Everton, who started the day on 41 points, or Sheffield United, Ipswich or Saints, all on 42 points.

In front of a crowd of nearly 27,000 at Upton Park, we went through every possible emotion. We had to hold our nerve when we went behind early on, and had to stay in the game and make sure we did not concede a second. Matt equalised with a free-kick, just before half time, and Neil Maddison headed us in front from one of Matt's crosses, but we were pegged back again at 2–2. Then Matt scored a penalty, his second goal of the game and his 25th goal of the Premier League season.

Whenever he stood over a free-kick or penalty, I had complete faith in him. There was never any doubt in my mind that he would score. That day at West Ham was no different. Matt's penalty put us in front with about 25 minutes to go. I had seen him do it so often over the years and he was in perhaps the best form of his entire career.

We were 3–2 up when West Ham fans invaded the pitch in what seemed to be a fit of end-of-season exuberance mixed in with the fact they were losing. The first I knew about it was when our goalkeeper Dave Beasant charged past me shouting, 'Ruuuuuuuuun!' I will never forget the sight of his tall frame lumbering towards the tunnel.

We had been defending the old North Bank at Upton Park, known in those days as the Centenary Stand. I was on the opposite side of the pitch to the tunnel and close to the stand they called the Chicken Run, home to some of the most ardent West Ham supporters. Once, on another occasion, I had gone to retrieve a ball from the Chicken Run and instead of throwing the ball back, someone threw an entire raw chicken at me. It landed by me at the side of the pitch. I'm just pleased I didn't catch it.

As stewards tried to clear the home fans from the pitch, we were back in the away dressing room and other scores were filtering in from around the country. Everton had fought back from 2–0 down to win. Sheffield United had lost to a late goal at Chelsea and were going down unless we conceded three goals in the last few remaining minutes and somehow lost 5–3.

We went back out to finish the game. The West Ham fans had been ushered from the pitch but were standing on the edge, crowded tightly around the touchline on the perimeter track. Ken Monkou headed into his own goal to make it 3–3 and triggered another invasion and we all raced down the tunnel again. This time we did not return.

I'm sure there still was a minute or two of stoppage time to be played but referee Gerald Ashby decided enough was enough. The game was over, he said, and there were no complaints from our dressing room. We were safe and, amid the jubilation, high-fives and handshakes there was an overriding sense of relief. It had been so tense for so many weeks with so much riding on us staying in the Premier League.

Matt and I embraced and shared a quiet moment. He had scored eight goals in our last four games. We realised what it meant not just to us as players and as people but, also, to the club and the community. Who knows what would have happened had we gone down with the Premier League in its infancy. We knew it would not be easy to bounce back, just as Sheffield United, Oldham and Swindon discovered.

* * *

When Bruce Grobbelaar joined us on a free transfer from Liverpool in the summer of 1994 nobody was expecting it to be boring. He was a goalkeeper of real pedigree, having won everything worth winning in 14 years at Anfield, and came with a reputation as a larger-than-life character.

On the pitch, you were never quite sure what Bruce was going to do. There was one game when I found him almost overlapping me on the wing and I wondered what the hell was going on.

He made his debut for Saints in August and was engulfed by a match-fixing scandal before the end of November. *The Sun* newspaper claimed they had video evidence of Bruce agreeing to fix games with a betting syndicate in Asia. John Fashanu and Hans Segers of Wimbledon were also accused. They all denied the allegations.

I had never heard of anything to do with match-fixing. News reporters and camera crews besieged us at the training ground. We were not used to intrusions like this at Southampton. Even when we retreated to the most secluded pitches we heard rustling in the trees and turned to see a line of lenses appear over the top of the fence.

It was a huge national story. I found it strange that Bruce did not want to address the players about it. If it had been me in that position, wrongly accused, I would have felt the urge to come in and say, 'Look guys, it's not true, it's a pack of lies, I want you to hear it from me.' It would have been good to hear him say that. When you are in a team, a band of brothers fighting for the same goal, you cannot have any doubts about those alongside you. To my knowledge, that did not happen. I never heard Bruce address the squad on the matter and he never mentioned it personally to me. I guess everyone has their own way of dealing with things.

He must have been under immense personal pressure but he just continued to train and play and behave in the same way. Perhaps that is testament to his concentration. Southampton fans were supportive. Some waved fake money at him and he laughed along and made light of the situation. Alan Ball kept him in the team. The first game after the story broke was Arsenal at home. He kept a clean sheet amid the frenzy and we won 1–0.

We lurched into trouble in mid-season but we recovered and put together a good run of form to finish in 10th spot. Bruce rarely played during the next season. He left us to join Plymouth and we followed his trials from afar. He was cleared of the match-fixing allegations in 1997 although the legal actions continued for years.

* * *

This was the time when I was feeling most secure about my place in the team. I was never totally at ease, but I was established in the team under Ian Branfoot and playing regularly under Bally. We were winning games and seemed to be moving the club in the right direction again.

Then came the bombshell – Bally left us for Manchester City. I felt as if we were back at square one again. It was a big disappointment, made a little easier for me personally because Dave Merrington was his replacement. Dave had been my youth team manager and a massive influence over so many of us at that level. He moulded us as people and footballers.

But it must have been difficult for him, stepping up to impose his style on a group of senior pros, a lot of them set in their own ways. Our one season under Dave turned into another close shave with relegation but we produced some good performances and big results, just when we needed them.

Manchester United were six points clear at the top of the Premier League when they came to The Dell in April 1996. They had a formidable line-up. Eric Cantona, Roy Keane, Andy Cole, Ryan Giggs and David Beckham were all in the team. We were just two points above the relegation zone with four games remaining. Goals had been a problem for us but we scored three in the first half. Ken Monkou scored the first after about 10 minutes, Neil Shipperley put us 2–0 up, sweeping it in, and Matt Le Tissier got the third just before half time. Peter Schmeichel came for a high cross and parried it down to Matt, who flicked it back across the keeper and slotted it in.

It was a perfect 45 minutes from our point of view. The early goal helped set the tone. When the big clubs came to The Dell in those days, we always tried to start in an intense fashion, getting in and among them, with the supporters behind us. We had a feeling they didn't like playing there and we knew we were capable of causing a bit of an upset at home. Still, we had not expected to go in at half time with a 3–0 lead. We had not scored three in a Premier League match since the opening game of the season, when we lost a 4–3 thriller at home to Nottingham Forest. We felt in complete control but, even with a healthy lead, we were wary of United's ability to mount a comeback.

We were 10 minutes into the second half when it dawned on me that they were now wearing different colour shirts, which goes to show how poor my powers of observation are. They were now playing in blue -and -white shirts, having changed out of the grey shirts with white shorts and white socks they had started the match in. Only then did I start to think how odd that was.

I didn't ask any of the United players about it as I didn't really go in for pleasantries. That sort of interaction wasn't me. I did interact once or twice with opponents but it tended to be more actions than words. I certainly wasn't going to say, 'Oh, excuse me, why have you changed your kit?' My mind was concentrating on the game. The only thought that popped into my head was that United were at the forefront of football's new commercialisation. They regularly released new kits, and I thought this must be another marketing gimmick, advertising two different shirts in one game.

That was a stupid thing to do, I thought, as the second half played itself out. We won 3–1. Giggs pulled a goal back near the end but we kept them at bay. Then, not long after the final whistle, we started to hear about some of the comments Sir Alex Ferguson was making to the media, claiming his players had been unable to see each other clearly in their grey shirts and that was the reason they had changed colours. It was different, I'll give him that.

I couldn't keep the smile from my face. It's true, with the crowd so tight around the pitch at The Dell that it could be difficult to pick players out, but mostly this applied to Saints players – thousands of fans in the crowd wore identical shirts to me and my teammates. We were the ones who blended in, so I couldn't understand how United struggled to see their grey shirts against the sea of red and white in the crowd.

It was disappointing Sir Alex couldn't just come out and say, 'Southampton were better than us.' We were rarely given any credit and that became a source of frustration over the years. It was always about why the bigger clubs had had an off day and lost, rather than how well Saints had done.

We beat Manchester United three years in a row at The Dell. This was the first, then we beat them 6–3 when they came back six months later, and won 1–0 in January 1998, when Kevin Davies scored the only goal.

The grey shirts win, however, was a big three points for us in our relegation battle. United went on to win the title with some ease and complete the Double. We lost our next game at Newcastle and then won 1–0 at Bolton, with a goal from Matt, and went into the final game of the season, Wimbledon at home, in need of a win to be sure of survival.

Bolton and QPR were already down, and we were locked together on points with Coventry and Bally's Manchester City. Coventry's goal difference was better than ours, and ours was better than City's.

It was tense and scrappy but I never thought we were in trouble against Wimbledon. They were safe in mid-table with nothing much to play for and we heard City were trailing 2–0 in their game against Liverpool. You were always within earshot of the fans, or a member of staff if you were on the side of the dug-outs. I would ask the fans, 'Where are we? What do we need to do?'

All the drama and confusion on that day came at Maine Road. Manchester City fought back to level at 2–2 and for a time they thought that was enough to mean they were safe when actually they weren't. Everything became much closer than we realised. Another goal for City against Liverpool and we would have been sent down but that goal never came. We played out a goalless draw with Wimbledon. Coventry drew 0–0 with Leeds. City drew 2–2. We all finished the season on 38 points but City went down on goal difference.

On a personal note, I did feel a little for Bally. I knew what it meant to him. We stayed up at City's expense, and in a way we were a team he had built. That is football, and that is the competitive element of the game. We stayed up and that was the main thing.

* * *

Football's ruthless edge had never really bothered me, although it did seem especially harsh when Dave Merrington was sacked at the end of the season. He had kept us afloat in the Premier League at a time when his wife, Pauline, had been seriously ill and Dave must have been under a great deal of stress. He largely kept Pauline's illness from the players because he didn't want to bring his personal concerns into the club. He was focused and truly professional, but the thanks he received was to lose his job. I was very sad. I had played the bulk of the games that season. I knew him as well as anybody in the dressing room and I liked him.

What's more, for as long as I could recall, Southampton had been the epitome of stability. Ted Bates was the manager for 18 years from 1955. His statue now stands outside St Mary's Stadium in tribute to his work leading Saints out of Division Three (South) and establishing them as a top-flight club in the old Division One.

When Ted stepped aside, he handed the reins to his assistant, Lawrie McMenemy. Lawrie was in charge for 12 wonderful years. He was replaced by Chris Nicholl, who was a former Southampton player returning to the club, and he stayed in the role for six years.

From this point on, the position became highly unstable and we seemed to be changing the manager every year or two, for different reasons. First, Ian Branfoot, Alan Ball and Dave Merrington, all with links to Southampton. Then we moved in a different direction with the appointment of Graeme Souness. There is a strong argument to say the non-stop chopping and changing of managers does not help the development of a team, but I feel fortunate to have played under some of the great characters of the game, some great coaches. I was able to learn something from them all and I will always be grateful to them.

When I discovered Graeme was coming in as manager, I could not help but feel excited. He had been a magnificent midfielder for Liverpool and Scotland. I had stood a few times on the Kop at Anfield as a boy and watched him with my cousins.

As a manager, he had been in charge of three enormous clubs with huge appeal: Rangers, Liverpool, and Galatasaray in Turkey. His appointment was a departure for Saints, a bold move, and I thought it would be very interesting to work with him.

Graeme was a feisty character, not unlike myself, but the warmth of my feelings cooled when a flurry of summer signings included a new left-back, Graham Potter. Then we went to Scotland for preseason and I wasn't starting the games.

These were always among the toughest times. I was established in the first team, I had fought to protect our status as a Premier League club and a new management team turned up with new ideas. They signed a player specifically for my position. They did not exactly say, 'We don't like you and what you do,' but they might as well have done because that is how it felt.

This happened to me quite a few times over the course of my career. New managers did not know me as a person. They did not know my character or my devotion to the club. But they had perceptions of me, and they all thought they knew someone who could do a better job at left-back because one of the first things they did when they arrived was to go out and sign one.

Southampton paid £250,000 for Graham Potter from Stoke when Graeme arrived in 1996. A few years earlier, we paid £350,000 for Simon Charlton from Huddersfield, although we did play quite a few games together, with Simon in midfield. Later, when Dave Jones came in as manager, his first move was to sign Lee Todd, a left-back who he worked with at Stockport.

I had been club captain for a couple of years when Dave was appointed in 1997, and was asked to pop down to The Dell and make myself available for interviews on the day when he was unveiled before the media as our new manager. I met Dave, we shook hands and said hello and exchanged pleasantries. Then, without a word of warning, the club signed Lee for £850,000 and gave him my number three shirt. I was demoted to the number 15 shirt. That was a real kick in the teeth. Dave Jones also went on to sign Patrick Colleter and John Beresford, and they were left-backs, too. It's fair to say that Dave really wasn't sure about me.

These were my back-to-square-one moments. Managers were coming and going, the transfer market was starting to turn over more quickly and these factors signalled changes in my fortunes. Within the broader fight to avoid relegation, I was fighting my personal survival battles and frustrated by selection issues. They tested my temper at times. I might take it out on my teammates in a training session or snap back at the manager and tell him I wanted to play. One thing I was not going to do was to kick the manager's door down and tell him I wanted to leave.

I did not ever want to leave Southampton. I was a boy from the city, and was settled with Karen and the children. I had no desire to uproot my family. We were in the top flight and I just wanted to stay and play for the club I loved. The contracts I signed probably reflected that but I never signed anything I wasn't happy with.

Football to me was about more than just money so whenever my position came under threat, my response was to get my head down and set about fighting my way back into the team. I like to think the managers came to understand what I was like. They saw the way I applied myself and lived my life, the way I trained, and the qualities I brought to the group and the squad. I was always ready to back myself. I refused to be daunted even though the world of football was changing rapidly.

Money came flooding into the game after the creation of the Premier League and the quality of the cars in the players' car park gradually started to improve. Barry Venison was the first of the new breed at Southampton. He joined us in 1995, and his souped-up BMW with its personalised number plate made everyone stop and stare.

Until this point, players were happy to drive an Escort XR3i or a Golf GTI but then we were off towards the super cars, first with convertible BMWs and, by the time I retired, we had players driving around in Ferraris and Lamborghinis, or travelling by private jet or helicopter. I certainly wasn't on that pay grade.

Carlton Palmer came in one day telling us he was off to the races with David Hirst after training. The racing was at Cheltenham and we were all wondering how on earth they were going to make it in time. We were still training when the helicopter started to circle us. Carlton said, 'Hirsty, the taxi's here.' It landed inside the training ground, and they scarpered at the end of the session, changed into three-piece suits, jumped into the helicopter and off they went.

* * *

The proportion of signings from overseas steadily increased, but this was not entirely new. I remember watching Yugoslavs Ivan Golac and Ivan Katalinic playing for Saints when I was growing up and, under Chris Nicholl, we signed Alex Cherednik and Sergey Gotsmanov from the former USSR.

Alex came first, followed by Sergey, who had been at Brighton. Alex was a strong right-back and Sergey was a winger and one hell of an athlete. I was fit and often at the front in any running drills but I was blown away by Sergey in a preseason cross-country run.

Ken Monkou, a Dutch defender who joined us from Chelsea in 1992, must go down as one of our best signings of the era. I often played alongside him, either as his partner in central defence or with me at left-back and Ken as the centre-half on my side. He was a real gentle giant off the pitch and he has remained a close friend.

Southampton also had good links with Norway. Claus Lundekvam and Egil Ostenstad were astute signings made under Graeme Souness. Tore Andre Flo came on trial with Egil but we couldn't afford him and he ended up at Chelsea.

Flo lined up against us on Boxing Day in 1999, when Gianluca Vialli selected a Chelsea team made up of 11 non-British players. This was a first in English football. The decade was about to end and the trend was well set.

Egil was a fine goalscorer and Claus became a fantastic servant who went on to have a testimonial at the club. We called him Silky because of the calm and skilful way he could bring the ball out of defence. He reminded me a lot of Alan Hansen. Equally, he wasn't afraid to put his head in where it would hurt and was often willing to patch-up and play with an injury. We still catch up occasionally when he is back in Southampton, and Karen and I met up with him a couple of years ago when we flew to his hometown of Bergen to pick up a cruise.

I played with Claus for many years. He formed some brilliant partnerships over the years with Ken Monkou, Dean Richards (whose untimely passing after illness at the age of 36 in 2011 was a huge loss), and Michael Svensson, who we nicknamed Killer, because he was one of those you stayed away from in the training games. Killer was as tough as they came and never shied away from an encounter with an opponent. Off the pitch, he is a real gentleman, quiet and mild-mannered.

Anders Svensson and Antti Niemi came from Scandinavia and did well for us, and we started to see players from further afield and the style of football shifted. Eyal Berkovic, an Israel international, was a talented footballer, and Hassan Kachloul, a Morocco international, was a wonderful player and a free spirit. Hassan would often play on the left in front of me and it could be an absolute nightmare trying to get him to help out defensively. His idea of football was just about going forward, attacking and trying to score goals.

In the middle of a game, he would turn around to me and say, 'Franny, why do you do this? Why are you kicking the ball in the air, straight up to the strikers? Why are we going so long? Come on, let's play, this is football, we play it on the ground, pass the ball to my feet.' I'd go, 'Yeah, OK mate, to feet next time.'

We signed Marian Pahars from Latvia. Nobody knew much about him except he was supposed to be Latvia's answer to Michael Owen. He was small in stature, very quick and could score goals for fun. I will never forget his goal against Manchester United at Old Trafford when he poked the ball through Jaap Stam's legs and smashed it into the net. He was such a fantastic player and has since gone on to manage his national team, which I would never have predicted. I didn't think he was the type of player who would want to stay in the game past his playing days.

Marian was my roommate when he came to the club and we got on well. He didn't have the mentality of some players when it came to injuries. If he had a cold, it was the flu. If he had a slight knock, it was a major injury. He questioned his own ability at times. I'd tuck him up in bed and tell him how good he was.

As club captain, I was often paired with the new signings to help them settle. I roomed with Jeff Kenna in my early days (we still call each other 'Roomie'), with Matt Le Tissier for a time, and with Gordon Watson when he was signed from Sheffield Wednesday.

Gordon joined us for the first time at the hotel ahead of an away game. I had been told to expect him and there was a knock at the door. I said, 'Hey, Gordon, nice to meet you, welcome.' He just walked in, straight past me and said, 'Call me Flash.'

He wasn't short of confidence. Within half an hour, Flash was lighting a cigarette, opening a window and saying, 'You don't mind if I smoke do you, Franny? I'll do it out of the window, here.' I said, 'Yes, I do mind actually Flash, get outside.' I've always had a soft spot for Flash and our friendship lasted far beyond our playing days. He's a great character but we didn't last long as roommates. I liked to sleep a lot and he was hyperactive.

* * *

The 1996–97 season under Graeme Souness turned into another serious scrap for survival. We were bottom of the league with only five games remaining but it was very tight and we were producing our usual springtime flourish by the time we came up against Coventry at The Dell in April.

We were 2–0 up and looking good for three more points when my mistake let them back into the game. I under-hit a pass to goalkeeper Maik Taylor and Peter Ndlovu nipped in to score. The game swung on the goal. We couldn't hold out, Noel Whelan equalised and we had to settle for a point.

I was so disappointed. My slip had cost us and the pressure was on with only three to play. I didn't need Graeme to march into the dressing room and spell it out. 'That's cost us,' he said. He was fuming at me. 'We're going down because of you.' I didn't react well. I jumped straight up to my feet and confronted him. We didn't come to blows but I certainly wasn't happy.

I was always self-critical. The last thing I ever needed was for a manager, teammate, supporter or anyone in my family to tell me when I had performed poorly or done something wrong. I knew. I could be quite vocal in the dressing room and maybe I was a bit quieter when I had a shocker.

It was a side issue but this was my testimonial year and we had a match arranged, two days after the end of the season. I was horrified by the prospect that this might be the year when we actually went down. Even worse if people were blaming me. I could not imagine being in a position where I was expecting fans to come along to see a match to celebrate my career in those circumstances.

Just three days after the Coventry game we were up at Sunderland. It was another six-pointer with the losers almost sure to go down. Unhappily, I was dropped to the bench but early in the game Claus Lundekvam dislocated his shoulder and I was sent on.

I was determined to make amends and managed to perform well as we won 1–0 against an experienced Sunderland side, which included the attacking prowess of Niall Quinn, Chris Waddle and Paul Stewart. Emotions were running high because it was the penultimate match for them at Roker Park before the move to the Stadium of Light, and this defeat virtually condemned them to relegation.

It was a massive result for us and personally very satisfying for me. Of course, I didn't want us to be relegated, and I certainly didn't want to be relegated with the manager thinking my mistake against Coventry was the reason for it. It was nice to bounce back. I wasn't pleased to see Claus injured but I was back in the team and this result gave us the impetus to stay up again.

I kept my place for the next game as we beat Blackburn and this win virtually secured our survival. Graeme didn't hold any grudges. We all say things in the heat of the moment and it was nice to prove I could be of some help.

We lost at Aston Villa, on the final day. It was our only defeat in the last eight games of the season and thankfully proved irrelevant. We finished a point clear of danger as Sunderland, Middlesbrough and Nottingham Forest went down.

* * *

The greatest of all our 'Great Escapes' was still to come, this one under Dave Jones, after Graeme Souness had resigned amid reports of a disagreement with our new chairman Rupert Lowe.

In our first season under Dave, we finished in the relative comfort of 12th spot but we made an atrocious start to his second. We lost the first five games and were firmly entrenched at the bottom of the league with only two points when we went to Coventry on 24 October and won for the first time. Our form improved but we spent almost the entire season in the bottom three and nothing looked like changing as we trailed 3–1 with an hour gone at home to Blackburn in April.

Blackburn were one of our rivals near the bottom and we conjured up a fightback. Mark Hughes pulled a goal back for us and Marian Pahars made it 3–3 in the 81st minute. It was Marian's first goal for the club and it boosted our confidence.

We ground out a goalless draw at Derby and then beat Leicester 2–1 on 1 May, with goals from Chris Marsden and James Beattie, to climb out of the relegation zone for the first time all season.

There were two games left and next up was a trip to Wimbledon at Selhurst Park. They were a club without a home at the time, sharing at Crystal Palace and unable to attract crowds big enough to fill the stadium. It meant the away allocation was always bigger than at any other fixture and an estimated 12,000 Southampton supporters made the trip up the M3 to London for the game.

It felt like a home game from the moment we stepped out of the tunnel and saw a mass of red and white on the other side of the stadium. It was as though we were being cheered to safety. Just as anxiety in the crowd can be contagious and spread to the players, on that day the party atmosphere and the supreme confidence among the Saints fans, with everyone singing along to the *Great Escape* theme tune, gave me a feeling of invincibility.

We rode our luck at times. Our goalkeeper Paul Jones made a couple of good early saves and I was able to block a shot from Robbie Earle on the line just before half time, when the score was still 0–0. There was a loud appeal for handball. I fear it may have been a penalty if VAR technology was around in those days, because it did strike my arm. It wasn't obvious in the sense that I didn't stick my hand out to make a save. Instead, I leaned forward into the shot and we scrambled the ball clear. I was pleased to make an important contribution and we all knew it would be very tough if we went a goal behind.

Matt Le Tissier had been struggling with an injury and was ruled not fit enough to start the game, but he was among the substitutes and came on to create the first goal for James Beattie in the 72nd minute. Matt swung over a free-kick and James headed into the net. Then Matt scored directly from a corner to make it 2–0 with the slightest deflection off Robbie Earle at the near post. Our fans erupted and we all sprinted over to bundle on top of Matt. Suddenly, staying up looked a distinct possibility, which no one would have predicted given our dreadful form over the season.

Our hopes were boosted a few days later when Blackburn were relegated following a draw against Manchester United. Nottingham Forest were already down. The final place was between us and Charlton. We were two points better off but they had a much better goal difference, so we still had to beat Everton at The Dell to be certain of survival. We did it quite comfortably with two goals from Marian Pahars in a 2–0 win. Charlton lost at home to Sheffield Wednesday and we ended up with a cushion of five points, which was a deceptive degree of comfort.

We had done it again. We escaped by winning our last three games. Victory at Wimbledon was the key moment and survival was more important than ever, since it triggered plans for a new stadium. We celebrated staying up at The Dell while also facing up to the idea of leaving our beloved home.

5

CULT CLASSIC

'Franny won the fans over because he was Mr Reliable. With Southampton more often than not fighting relegation they needed people to stick together and he was totally committed. He had the right attitude. He was dedicated and wanted to learn his craft – and his stamina was unbelievable.

We'd do a bleep test to check our fitness levels on the first day of preseason, running back and forth between two lines, keeping in time with the bleeps, which became quicker. I'd dip out at one of the early stages because I knew I would be expected to beat it next week. Old head, you see.

Franny just ran and ran until he was the last one standing. He was one of the best I'd seen. Terry McDermott could run but he drank a lot. Franny didn't drink, which was a rarity at the time. He was a perfect gent. Whenever people ask me how come I was still playing in Division One in my late 30s, I tell them it was down to the likes of Franny.'

Jimmy Case, Southampton player 1985–91

Matt Le Tissier was, quite rightly, the player Southampton fans adored. We came through the ranks at the same time and they took to him instantly. Why wouldn't they? With me, it took time. I had to work hard on the supporters before I was able to win them over.

Maybe I wasn't able to convince every single one of them. I dare say there will have been some who didn't like me as a player from my first game to my very last. Technically, I wasn't the best player they saw, but I do think quite a few of them recognised my effort and determination, my passion and desire, and maybe they came to respect my loyalty and commitment to the club over time.

I am always humbled by the details supporters can remember about my career, and genuinely amused and touched by the 'Benali on Tour' craze started a few years ago by some Saints fans who took to fixing old Panini stickers of me from the mid-90s in curious places around the world and sharing pictures on social media platforms.

Football fans are notorious for their banter, and the Twitter account set up for 'Benali on Tour' tweets some hilarious photographs. I've been sent photos of my face stuck in all sorts of random locations around the world. I'm reliably informed there's one on Brooklyn Bridge in New York, on the Christ the Redeemer statue in Rio de Janeiro and somewhere along the Great Wall of China. Toilet blocks are always popular spots for a sticker, especially inside football grounds, pubs and service stations.

My phone will occasionally chime with a message from a friend or colleague who wants to tell me they've seen my face pasted up inside the San Siro or at Sparta Prague. One of my favourites was a picture of someone in a Portsmouth shirt with four Benali stickers on his back. No Pompey fan I know will have been happy about that.

I used to love collecting Panini stickers when I was a young boy obsessed by football and always thought how cool it must be for a player to feature in an album, and swapped by young fans in the school playground.

My son Luke would have been about five years old when he started to collect them. One day, Karen was helping him to open a few packets when she found my familiar features staring out from inside the wrapper. She was excited and keen to see Luke's reaction as he eagerly went through hoping to find one of the players he was missing. He snapped up the card and shouted out 'swap' as he put me on his swap pile. Karen laughed, rescued me from the swaps and said, 'I don't think we need to swap daddy.'

It was around this time when figurines of Premier League footballers came out, made by Corinthian. They were cool little things and we still have a couple of Benali ones at home. I usually find one pushed into the centre of a cake on my birthday. As for the stickers, there are probably more of me stuck up around the toilet blocks of the world with the 'Benali on Tour' craze than were ever collected and stuck into albums.

I see it as a great compliment. I love my close connection with the Saints fans. If they consider me to be some sort of a cult hero then I am honoured. I have always seen it as my responsibility to represent them because I came from the city and developed through the youth ranks. I was out there in a Southampton shirt, with the badge on my chest and occasionally with the captain's armband on my arm.

It became a big part of me and the way I thought. I counted myself fortunate to be out on the pitch and I gave it everything. Never less than 100 per cent. I fought for my team and the fans. Sometimes quite literally.

I wanted to be as good as I could be. I wanted to help Southampton win games and to be a Premier League club and, over the years, I think that's what endeared me to them. But I certainly had my share of critics.

* * *

Early in my career, I was in the team at The Dell and I wasn't playing particularly well. My passing was a little awry and there was a section of the supporters in the East Stand getting on my back. One voice pierced through the hum of the crowd. Every time I missed my target with a pass, I heard him, and thought he must be sitting among the long benches we had in the days before the stadium was all-seater. 'Hey Benali, any chance you can find someone in red and white today?'

I tried to play another ball up the line. Again, it did not go to my intended target. It was cut out and bounced away, into the advertising boards. As I went to collect it, there was the voice again. I looked up into the benches. One gentleman was standing up and shouting insults at me, telling me I was this and that. I looked at him and made eye contact. Normally I would have ignored him and got on with it but inside I was boiling.

I'd been coming in for a bit of criticism from a few of the supporters. I grabbed the ball and kicked it towards him. Not intending to hurt him of course. Just to shut him up. Typically, it swerved away, missing by some distance. It disappeared into the crowd. It was just one of those days. He held out his hands and looked around to the other fans as if to say, 'There you go everybody, I rest my case.'

The ball came back to me and I got on with the game as quickly as I could. I was still fuming inside. That was exactly the sort of thing that got under my skin and there were times when I reacted.

In a home game against Leeds there was another similar exchange. I was playing with a bandage on my hand because I had snapped a tendon in the ring finger on my left hand, pulling at someone's shirt as I defended. I know how that sounds but this little thing had caused me such intense pain. I had an operation to fix it and it was made clear that this would be an operation they could only do once. If it snapped again then it would be something I would just have to put up with and the tendon would shrivel away up my arm.

For what seemed to be ages, I had to play in a cast covered in a bandage, which meant I wasn't able to grapple and hold onto players, which I always liked to do, especially when I was marking at a set-piece.

This was one of the games in the cast and it hadn't gone well. I was walking off towards the tunnel in the corner of The Dell, towards the stairs with home fans on both sides of me. I seemed to be bearing the brunt of the criticism from one particular supporter. He was giving me all sorts of grief. I'd probably had a poor game but I could do without this.

I trudged from the pitch, with my eyes down and unravelling my bandage and all I could hear was abuse coming from this guy. I glanced up and saw him just as the bandage became completely unwound. I rolled it tightly into a ball and flung it at him in disgust. This time my aim was better and he had a souvenir to take home.

It was hurtful to come in for such personal criticism. I was the local lad and sometimes that makes it easier for them to make you the target. I saw several talented young players over the years who came through the system and broke into the team, only for their confidence to be shot to pieces by this sort of treatment from sections of the crowd.

I was determined not to let it happen to me. Just as I was always trying to prove my worth to the different managers, I thought I was fighting to win approval from the supporters as well. At least some of them.

When the cast finally came off and I was able to grapple freely once again, the same tendon snapped again in the very first game. It was just as painful as it was the first time and, now, impossible to repair and I have never since been able to move that finger fully.

Overall, I consider myself fortunate with injuries. I didn't have too many bad ones but another came when I broke my arm playing at Leicester in December 1998. I managed to play on for the last 30 minutes of the game but I was in agony. I had sprinted at full speed and jumped up to win a header with my forearm raised, for protection more than anything else, and clattered into the back of Andy Impey's head.

I had a good idea from the instant shooting pains that something was badly damaged, but was determined not to go off injured. To go off, I thought, would be letting down my team and the supporters so I struggled on to the end. I can still picture the confused look on Matt

Oakley's face when I tried taking a throw-in to him. The ball landed closer to my own feet than it did to his.

The doctor confirmed the injury in the dressing room. He pressed his fingers into my arm and had to peel me off the ceiling. Yes, definitely broken. I had an operation with a metal plate and seven screws inserted to fix the break. A few weeks later, I was at home recovering and able to do some fitness exercises without taking part in any contact sessions. There was no pain or discomfort any longer and I thought the bone must have healed. I did not expect any problems when I decided to go outside and rake a load of leaves from the lawn.

That night, however, the same forearm was aching once again. Southampton sent me for x-rays and found the plate had snapped. The raking motion had caused it to twist and break. I had to go back for another operation and have a stronger plate fitted, which delayed my recovery. This plate is still inside my arm and the original is in a glass bottle in my desk drawer.

Years later, towards the end of my career, I suffered a hairline fracture in a leg in a training collision with Kevin Davies, who was known as the 'Tank' for good reason. It kept me out for a while in preseason but that was about the worst of it.

* * *

After a difficult start, the supporters slowly warmed to my style. The tackle on John Fashanu at Wimbledon proved to be something of a catalyst. The red card obviously didn't help my teammates but it did seem to endear me to a few fans. Maybe they liked the fact I didn't really care who the opposition were. I didn't care much for reputations. They would all come in for the same sort of treatment from me.

Maybe they came to realise I was one of them. I loved the Saints. I loved to represent my home city and, like them, I wasn't particularly keen on Portsmouth, our fierce rivals from 19 miles along the coast.

The strength of animosity between Southampton and Pompey is probably one of those you don't totally appreciate until you live in the area. Alan Ball always said the hostility was no less intense than it was between Everton and Liverpool, or Manchester City and United.

For me, it carried on beyond my playing career. When I was running my son Luke's team, we came up against teams from that neck of the woods and there were times when people refused to shake my hand after a match.

I will sometimes opt out of a shopping trip with Karen to Gunwharf Quays, near Portsmouth, because I know what it might entail and yet, when I came to embark on the endurance challenges for Cancer Research UK, there were so many kind comments and generous donations from Pompey fans. Some things I know can transcend the bitterest football rivalry.

* * *

In May 1993, I was touched when hundreds of Saints supporters paid me the great honour of making me the subject of their traditional fancy dress outing on the final away game of the season. Over the years they have worn fezzes for our Morocco international Hassan Kachloul, and ginger wigs and tartan bonnets for Gordon Strachan.

We were away at Oldham, who were in desperate need of the points to stay up. We lost 4–3, all our goals by Matt Le Tissier, at the end of a season when we almost crashed into relegation trouble with an awful run of six defeats in the last eight games. We were safe by the time we travelled to Oldham, who survived on goal difference thanks to the win. Crystal Palace lost at Arsenal and went down. Many of our fans were there in dark wigs, sunglasses and false moustaches. My teammates thought it was hilarious as our coach made its way through the streets to Boundary Park and we spotted more and more Saints supporters in fancy dress.

Kicking a ball about outside my first home at Albion Towers.

My first game at The Dell, in 1981, introducing England captain Kevin Keegan to the Southampton Schoolboys U.13s.

Preparing for a Wembley debut with England Schoolboys U.15s in March 1984, still a striker back then.

Early days in the Saints first team.

We are staying up, final-day celebrations at The Dell in May 1996.

6 June 1992 – had many teammates over the years but only one Soul Mate.

FRIENDS PROVIDENT
The Saints' choice for savings and pensions

Saints team photo 2002–03 featuring star signings Luke and Kenzie.

Celebrating Matt's sensational free-kick with Jeff Kenna at The Dell against Wimbledon on 26 February 1994. One of many!

PHOTOGRAPH COURTESY OF THE SOUTHERN DAILY ECHO

© BENALI FAMILY

© BENALI FAMILY

PHOTOGRAPH COURTESY OF THE SOUTHERN DAILY ECHO

Mini Me! In the dressing room with Luke on his first birthday, 7 July 1994.

Kenzie was born in 1995 and my team was complete. At home in 1998.

One of the greatest nights of my life, walking out for my testimonial with Luke, Kenzie and my niece Laura.

First season at St Mary's 2001–02, Matt's last at the club. With Luke and Kenzie.

So pleased to hand the reins to another local lad, Wayne Bridge.

Defending with Ken Monkou at Stamford Bridge against future teammate Dan Petrescu. Wearing Chelsea's away socks as club forgot to pack ours!

Best of enemies, the greatest striker Southampton ever produced – and Alan Shearer!

Winning the ball cleanly from David Beckham, Old Trafford, September 1999.

Tussling with Ryan Giggs at St Mary's, my final Premier League appearance, February 2003.

Ian Wright was probably my most difficult opponent.

I want to break free. Practising my best Freddie Mercury impression.

32,000 Benali masks for the Big Race finale at St Mary's on 16 October 2016.

Clocking up the miles through the Brecon Beacons on the Big Run in September 2014.

© BENALI FAMILY

Approaching St Mary's at the end of the Big Race.

© BENALI FAMILY

© BENALI FAMILY

Never a pleasurable way to finish every day of each challenge. This was Big Run at Turf Moor, Burnley.

PHOTOGRAPH COURTESY OF THE SOUTHERN DAILY ECHO

Jack Joslin was undergoing treatment for a brain tumour and this was an emotional moment at the finish line of the Big Run.

Final leg of Iron Fran through the New Forest with my cycling wing man Andrew Hartley, May 2019.

Swimming. The toughest discipline of Iron Fran.

Amazing party atmosphere for the Iron Fran homecoming at the Guildhall, Southampton.

Proudly celebrating more than £1 million raised for Cancer Research UK.

Media duties at Wembley with Jake Humphrey, Frank Lampard and Steven Gerrard.

My world.

Once a Saint always a Saint! Love my work as a speaker.

Honoured to win the JustGiving Celebrity Fundraiser of the Year award in 2015.

That moustache was a bit of a trademark from my early teens, it was something of a fashion statement in the 80s and it used to scare some of the defenders in schoolboy football. I decided to shave it off when Graeme Souness was appointed manager in the summer of 1997. The club simply wasn't big enough for two bristling moustaches so mine had to go. Karen had been telling me to get rid of it for years. It has not returned.

* * *

I was very proud to be made club captain by Alan Ball, and to serve in the role for the best part of a decade. Predominantly, it meant dealing with off-the-pitch matters, making sure there were players available for visits to schools and hospitals around the city. It was always a big part of what we stood for as a club and I enjoyed doing it. There might be a few moans and groans to take upstairs to the chairman and the bonus sheet to sort out every season, with incentives for where we finished in the league and cup competitions, or to make a case for the guys if they were looking for the occasional end of season trip. When Matt Le Tissier and Jason Dodd were unavailable there were times when I was asked to lead the team out, and that was always a special honour for me.

My duties as club captain would sometimes extend to providing a taxi service for the triallists and new signings. I lived quite close to the hotel where the club hired rooms for new players who did not have their own accommodation, and I would often pick them up on the way to training until they found their bearings.

It was November 1996 when I received a call from the club secretary asking if I could go to collect a player by the name of Ali Dia. Ali was with us for a trial, I was told, and he climbed into my car and gave me the now legendary George Weah story on the way to the training ground. Weah was one of the greatest players of his era, with an incredible career for AC Milan and Liberia. He was the World Footballer of the Year in 1995 and went on to become president of Liberia after retiring as a player.

When Ali said he was his cousin I took his word for it. It seemed feasible enough. I had no reason to doubt him, although the first of several bizarre twists came when a few of the lads were involved in a running session. Just as it started to step up and get tough Ali stopped and walked back to the changing rooms without a word. Ken Monkou and I looked at each other and then at the coach. No one said a word but we were all thinking the same thing. Why has he walked off? If you're trying to earn a contract you don't walk off. You do absolutely everything you can to impress.

He didn't stand out in training and was scheduled to play in a reserve game, which was cancelled. Then we reported on match day for a game against Leeds and Ali was there, in the dressing room at The Dell. One or two of us looked quizzically at each other. We thought he might be sitting in for the experience. Then the shirts were handed out he was among the substitutes. We knew we had injuries. We were light on the ground but this was quite a thing. No one even knew he had been registered.

Matt Le Tissier suffered an injury quite early in the game, which forced Graeme Souness to make a change and he sent on Ali. A half-chance came his way and he missed, and he ran around. I can't say I recall him being absolutely awful but the manager was obviously looking at it and thinking there was something not right, and decided to get him off. Ali was substituted, his Southampton career lasted 53 minutes and it has gone down in folklore.

It soon became clear afterwards that he wasn't really George Weah's cousin. He took off pretty sharpish and I never saw him again. The next I heard he was playing non-league football for Gateshead United. Everyone wanted to know how he had managed to pull off this ruse and appear in the Premier League. Graeme might not welcome the reminder.

I've always thought Ali Dia just happened to be in the right place at the right time.

* * *

My Testimonial Match in May 1997 was a great night of celebration. We had managed to complete another escape from relegation, which came as a relief, and our Southampton team were playing against a Lawrie McMenemy XI of former Saints players.

Alan Shearer and Tim Flowers came back and our manager Graeme Souness pulled on his boots and played. I couldn't have told you the score but the records have it down as an 8–7 win for Lawrie's team, and there was a full-house of more than 15,000 inside The Dell. It felt good to relax and have some fun with our fans after all those serious struggles we'd been through together.

Goalkeeper Dave Beasant played outfield in the first half, went up front and even scored a couple of goals. Amusingly, he then persuaded the paramedics from St John's Ambulance to carry him out on a stretcher for the start of the second half.

To see all those supporters there on that night in recognition of what I'd done at the football club until that point was incredible and the feeling of walking out onto the pitch with my son Luke and daughter Kenzie will live with me forever.

The fact I scored a goal with my right foot as well was equally memorable. I thought I might get the chance to take a penalty or someone might set me up with an easy chance, and so I was venturing forward a little more than I would normally have done. I picked the ball up on the left-hand side just outside the penalty box. I know I would have been closed down a bit quicker in a competitive game but no one closed me down so I cut inside and thought what the hell.

I struck one of the sweetest right-footers I have ever hit and it flew straight into the top corner past Tim Flowers. I have no doubt he was trying to stop it, he wasn't doing me any favours. I was 28 years old and, for someone who was initially signed up at the age of 14 as a prolific schoolboy striker, it did seem as though it had been quite a wait to show the Southampton fans I could score a goal.

There had been one or two for the reserves over the years. I scored a winner against Portsmouth in the Football Combination in September 1988, just before my first team debut, but I hadn't scored once in senior football. I must have struck my own version of a rich goalscoring seam because, having found the net in my Testimonial match, I went on to score my only competitive goal before the year was out.

It came in December 1997 at The Dell, against Leicester.

To this day, I have no idea what I was doing inside the Leicester penalty area for an attacking free-kick. There were very few occasions when I would go forward for a set-piece. I was decent in the air from a defensive point of view, but a combination of my poor goalscoring record and my good recovery speed meant I was usually one of those detailed to stay back and cover in case of any counter-attacks.

The fact that I hadn't scored by this stage of my career was a big talking point. I could feel the pressure every time I got into a position where I might shoot at goal and the supporters would often be shouting for me to have a go.

I hit the bar once at Tottenham and there was a moment early on in my career away against Derby when I went up for a header with Danny Wallace and we both got a touch. The ball flew in and the goal was credited to Danny. I knew I had touched it but I was a young lad and I knew it wasn't an argument I was going to win. Danny probably got the last touch anyway, but if I'd known back then how long I would be made to wait for a goal, I might have fought a bit harder for it.

On this occasion, we were 1–0 up against Leicester, and it must have seemed like a good idea at the time to drift forwards into the box as Matt Le Tissier prepared to deliver the free-kick from wide on the right.

The ball hurtled straight towards me and it never entered my mind to bring it down or take a touch. I just thought this is it. It was at a nice height to head. Just try to get a good connection on it and send it back across the goal.

It flew in off the bar. Silence hung over the stadium for a second or two. The entire ground was stunned into total disbelief, I imagine. I know I was. Then the place erupted. The supporters realised they had just witnessed something they thought they would never see. All the players bundled onto me as I stood there screaming at the crowd and they were screaming back.

Matt was the last player to reach me. We had been strike-partners in the youth team. He went on to score 209 goals for Southampton and this would be my only one. I didn't know it at the time but clearly there was no guarantee of more. He trotted over with a big smile on his face and we embraced as we made our way back to the halfway line. I said something like, 'I'm pleased it was you who set me up.'

Matt had scored the first goal of the game and Robbie Savage had pulled one back for Leicester. The win ended a run of four successive defeats, and I like to think mine was the important goal. There was relief from a personal perspective, similar to the emotions I experienced when we avoided relegation. At the very least, whatever else happened, I had managed to score once. It would end the talking point. And it was a half-decent goal, which was nice.

Our Christmas party was held the same night and, as the event went on, the comedian Stan Boardman, hired by Carlton Palmer as part of the entertainment, started calling people up onto the stage. He called up Carlton, Kevin Richardson, Terry Cooper (who was on the coaching staff) and, because I'd scored the goal, me.

We had no idea what Stan had in store for us once on stage but Karen was encouraging me to ditch my usual reserve and go for it. Typically, I dug my heels in and refused. I hate all that, I don't like being the centre of attention. And I'm so pleased I didn't get up because the

DJ gave all the boys a hat and expected them to strip off to one of the hits from the film *The Full Monty*. Some of them did. I would have been utterly mortified.

* * *

So 1997 proved to be the year of THE GOAL. I was delighted that it was Matt who had delivered the cross, and I was pleased he scored the other goal in what was an important win. I was also pleased it came at The Dell because the old place was dear to my heart. I walked past it as a boy on my way to school, stopping at the wooden gates without fail to gaze at the pitch and dream, and I came to know every inch of the place with its tight maze of corridors, its sounds and the smells, and the position of the sun at certain times of the day and year.

All these years later, I can close my eyes and picture it vividly. The entrance in the West Stand. The reception area and the boardroom. The old gym. Down a couple of steps, to the medical room on the left. Down another couple of steps into the corridor with the first-team dressing room on the right and the shower room on the left. Turn left for the away team dressing room. It was a bit smaller than the home dressing room but not the worst I'd seen. Outside the away team dressing room was a doorway leading to a narrow flight of stairs, like an old staircase you would find in a house. It could be quite a bottleneck. I remember having a brief scuffle with Paul Ince on those steps after a youth team game when we lost heavily to West Ham. Once you were down the staircase, you came down a slope in the corner and saw the stadium open up in front of you. That was always a great part of playing at The Dell. The pitch always seemed to be pristine and lush. I wasn't the biggest fan of the narrow cinder track around it because we'd run around it doing fitness sessions so many times as apprentices, but the pitch was a wonderful place to be.

The prospect of moving to the new stadium was an exciting step forward and for me there was a personal significance. Not only did the move take the club back to its roots in the heart of the city in St Mary's but it took me back to my roots, in the shadow of Albion Towers, my first home, where I lived with my mum and grandad.

Even so, I was sad to leave The Dell. So many of my footballing memories were entwined with the place. Night games under the lights were magical, and it was always a big advantage to Southampton. It helped us get results. Visiting teams didn't like it because it was tight and uncomfortable with our fans right on top of them, making a lot of noise. I've been to smaller grounds, such as Wimbledon's Plough Lane, and I've played in more hostile surroundings, such as the old Den at Millwall, where players came out through a cage and ran the gauntlet of all sorts of projectiles from the home fans but the atmosphere at The Dell enabled us to build intensity and generate momentum. If the ball went out of play, we could get it back in quickly and it meant we were able to get at teams, even the most prestigious ones, and unsettle them.

The last competitive game at the stadium was against Arsenal in May 2001. I was just back from Nottingham Forest, where I'd been on loan, and came off the bench for the last nine minutes. I'll always be grateful to Stuart Gray, who was our caretaker manager at the time. Stuart had been on the Saints coaching staff for many years in different roles and he knew how much it meant to both me and Matt Le Tissier to take part in that game.

So I'd been in Nottingham and Matt had been struggling all season with injuries. Stuart could easily have made his excuses but he told us that whatever happened we would be on the pitch at the final whistle and be part of the farewell because of the service we had given to the club over the years. He was true to his word. Matt played for a little bit longer than I did, and it worked out to be a great decision because he scored the winning goal in a 3–2 win. What could have been more fitting given all the goals we'd seen from him at The Dell?

One week later, there was an exhibition match against Brighton as a final sign-off. We won 1–0 as Uwe Rosler scored. I sat in the dressing room after the final whistle and listened to the noise from the stands as our supporters ripped out the seats. I walked around in a daze thinking I should take something as a keepsake but didn't take anything. I wish I had. Fixed up on the wall as you went down the steps from the dressing rooms towards the pitch there was an old sign which said, 'You are now entering The Dell'. That would have been nice to have. I left for home with nothing more than a piece of turf, which sat for a few years in a pot in the garden.

6

WAS THAT IT?

'Franny was Saints through and through. Always positive, always professional, he was the heart and soul of the club. When you're young and ambitious you don't appreciate you're taking someone else's place in the team, you just want to play. Then to hear Franny say he was happy that it was me who had taken his place, it made me quite emotional. I always get emotional when I think about Southampton.

I grew up watching them. Franny, Jason Dodd and Matt Le Tissier were all great players and I was quite nervous when I came into the team. I didn't have a lot of self-confidence. To have Franny there was amazing. I could tell he wanted me to do well. He never failed to speak to me. He worked so hard on his fitness and knew if I didn't work hard on mine he would always be there. He was always encouraging. He cared. He patted me on the back when I had done well and geed me up when I needed it.'

Wayne Bridge, Southampton player 1996–2003

It didn't take me long to work out I wasn't Glenn Hoddle's type of player and when I reached the end of my career and looked back I was convinced I could trace everything back to one game, a heavy defeat at Tottenham, not long after he arrived at Southampton. In fact, I think I could trace it back to just one half – the second half. Those 45 minutes at White Hart Lane marked the beginning of the end for me.

It was March 2000 and I didn't have a good game. We scored first but conceded four goals before half time and collapsed to a 7–2 defeat after the break. Glenn was quite critical of my performance and had a go at me for one of the goals in particular. I felt it at the time, but it was only looking back that I could identify the significance of the moment.

That must have been a painful defeat for him to take at Spurs, a club where he was revered as one of their greatest players, and he obviously thought I was a major part of what was an embarrassing result.

There was no meeting where he said, 'Look, Franny, you're not in my plans,' but actions spoke louder than words. From that point onwards, everything changed for me. I was dropped for the next game and only started two more matches in that season: a win at Bradford (a big three points), and a home defeat against Manchester United, which was another day to forget as they won the Premier League title again.

United went three goals up inside half an hour. They had won the Treble the previous season and that was probably the best team I faced in my career. David Beckham scored the first from a free-kick conceded by me for a foul on Andy Cole. That didn't go down well with Glenn. We all knew the dangers Beckham posed from free-kicks around the penalty area. Then I scored an own goal, to make it 2–0. I was trying to cut out a low cross from Phil Neville and turned it into the net at the near post. Ole Gunnar Solskjaer scored the third before Marian Pahars pulled one back for us.

I was hooked off at half time and that was my last appearance of the season. In fact, I only played a handful of games again and it would be almost three years before I started another game in the Premier League. My days as a Saints player were clearly numbered.

* * *

I often see Glenn when we are doing punditry work on TV. It is always nice to see him, and we get on really well but I cannot pretend his arrival at Southampton was a good development for my career.

Glenn replaced Dave Jones in unusual circumstances. In September 1999, Dave was charged with child abuse relating to a time when he worked at a school for children with behavioural problems in Merseyside in the 1980s. The case went all the way to Crown Court where it was dismissed immediately by the judge who made it clear Dave was innocent. The evidence was unreliable and it should never have gone that far.

By then, however, he had lost his job at Southampton. At first, it seemed as though the club were determined to stand by him. No one thought Dave was guilty and he was open and honest about the case. He would share what he could about its progress and told us categorically it wasn't true. I never doubted him.

I always liked Dave. True, I wasn't impressed when he first came in, took my squad number from me and gave it to Lee Todd without a word, but once I got to know him I liked him. There was no reason to dislike him, even though there were times when he wasn't selecting me and I thought I should be in the side. That was just the nature of the business. You always wanted to be in the team.

We won three of our first five games that season but went on a bad run in the weeks after Dave was charged and we slumped towards the relegation places. There was pressure on the board and a 5–0 defeat at Newcastle in January 2000 was probably the final straw.

Glenn came in with John Gorman as his assistant. They had been out of work since leaving the England job the previous year. Dave was placed on gardening leave, although it very soon became evident that Glenn's appointment was permanent. Dave would not be coming back to the club, and that must have been difficult for him and his family to accept.

Glenn was tactically very astute, not only when it came to our game plan, but also when he was talking about our opponents and tweaking things to try and stop them. But when Manchester United came on that day, he wanted us to sit off them and I thought that went against the way we always approached games at The Dell. Even against the big boys we liked to get at them, generate momentum and score some goals. We'd been successful playing this way against United in my time. It just didn't seem right to sit back and let them have the ball. It seemed to be very defensive. What's more, it didn't work.

Glenn's knowledge and tactical acumen might have been exceptional but you could not say the same about his man-management. He had been an outstanding player but we were not all blessed with the same natural talent, and his frustration at that was often apparent. Sometimes he would be looking for something either collectively or individually in a training session and we could not produce it.

One day we were crossing and shooting, and most of the squad were involved in a drill started by a bit of movement in midfield followed by a diagonal pass sprayed out wide to someone on the other side of the pitch. We weren't giving Glenn what he wanted so he stopped the session and said, 'This is what I'm after.' He flicked a ball up off the ground and pinged it 45 yards, right onto the toe of his intended target. It was a very good demonstration, especially considering he had not even warmed up and wasn't involved in the session – he had just been standing around. It just went to show his wonderful natural ability. Maybe it was a frustration for him that others couldn't do it, but it didn't always come across well. It was clear we weren't as good as he wanted us to be and he thought we should be better. That was something I felt at times and I know I wasn't the only one.

Other managers had made me feel like a champion able to take on and beat anybody. This wasn't the case with Glenn. The usual pattern would be for him to address the players and then leave. As soon as he was finished, John Gorman would move in trying to pick people up again. John was a contrast to Glenn and maybe that was the key to a successful partnership.

It's easy for me to be critical, I suppose, I went quite suddenly from being a regular for many years to being firmly on the outside. I wish it had been different. I would have loved to work with him more. I could have learned a lot from him but I had to contemplate leaving a club I had never wanted to leave.

First I was put among the subs, and if you're a defender you sit there knowing the best chance you have to get on is if someone is injured. Then I slipped further down the pecking order to just being in the squad – not even on the bench – and this hit me hard. Some players exist as squad players in the modern game and I often ask myself if I could handle that. They earn good money and maybe that makes it easier but I just wanted to play to satisfy my pride.

Football as I'd known it for many years was unlikely to ever return unless I left the club and dropped a division and that was never something I wanted to do. I always wanted to be at Southampton.

I had overcome similar challenges in the past, when new managers came in with new ideas and signed players to play specifically in my position but this time there was another element involved. Wayne Bridge was a wonderful young footballer emerging from the club's youth system. He was the future. And he was a left-back like me. This didn't bode well.

Confirmation of where I stood, if needed, came in the summer. We went on a closed-season training camp in La Manga in Spain. It was designed to boost our fitness during the break so that when we reported for preseason we had not been inactive for too long. We were in the final session on the final day when I nipped in to make a tackle in a small-side game. Kevin Davies was lining up a shot when I poked the ball away and he kicked the side of my lower-leg.

It turned out to be a hairline fracture. Not a bad break, but it was going to rule me out for most of the preseason. We came back from Spain and there was no call from Glenn to see how I was. Then we reported for the first day of preseason. I couldn't train with the first team but I had been doing a bit of fitness work when Glenn and I crossed on one of the paths at the training ground, Staplewood. As we passed each other, almost as an afterthought, Glenn turned and said, 'Oh, so you broke it then?' I wasn't after any special treatment but his comment did not make me feel wanted.

There was a setback when I opened up the fracture again playing for the reserves but once I was fully fit I started to think for the first time about a move on loan. I knew I wasn't going to play under Glenn but I was 30 years old and felt there was still a lot of football left in me. I had never contemplated the idea of leaving Southampton before. There was occasional speculation in the newspapers but I was never aware of another club making a bid or wanting to talk to me.

After I had retired, the former Wimbledon owner Sam Hammam told me he had once tried to buy me. He must have thought my style of play could have slotted in fairly well with the Crazy Gang but I didn't know anything about Wimbledon's interest at the time. I didn't want to know. I wasn't looking to leave and I didn't have an agent.

Once, towards the end of my career, there was a call from Kevin Bond, who was coaching at Portsmouth, to ask if I might be tempted into a move down the coast on loan. That was a very short conversation. Thanks but no thanks!

Reading showed an interest when it became clear I was looking to kick-start my career away from Southampton but I opted for a loan move to Nottingham Forest. They were in the second tier, Division One as it was at the time, but Forest is a big club with a rich history.

David Platt was the manager and we discussed the proposal on the phone. It was my first experience of a conversation with anyone really trying to tempt me to come to his club. He made me feel wanted, which was in stark contrast to the situation I was in at Saints. I was very quickly sold on the idea of a move to Forest, and the conversation with David was followed by a sombre family discussion with Karen and the children. Luke was seven years old at the time and Kenzie was five. We tried to explain I wouldn't be at home quite so often. It felt like a huge decision. I was signing on a one-month loan but it could easily turn into a permanent transfer. I didn't know if I would ever be coming back to Southampton.

Forest made me feel very welcome and looked after me. The former Saints goalkeeper Dave Beasant was there and he was a friendly face. They seemed ambitious about getting back into the Premier League. In the same week I signed, they paid £3.5 million for a new striker, David Johnson, from Ipswich. Jermaine Jenas made his league debut on my first appearance, against Crystal Palace in January 2001, and they had young talent coming through from the academy, like Andy Reid and Michael Dawson. At 34, David Platt was a young manager and, as with Glenn Hoddle, his quality was clear from his coaching demos. Once we were practising volleying, and his timing was so crisp and clean, I couldn't stop my mind flashing back to Italia 90 and his last-minute goal for England against Belgium, a volley dropping over his shoulder from a Paul Gascoigne free-kick.

The move to Nottingham Forest was a great experience, both in terms of football and in life. I'd always been the local lad who welcomed new players to Southampton. Suddenly I was a new face in the dressing room at a different club, seeing things from another angle. New club, new city, new supporters to win over. I was nervous but that was part of the appeal. I roomed with Riccardo Scimeca, a very friendly guy, and made my first connection with Steve Wigley, who finished his playing career on the south coast and was living in Southampton and coaching at Forest.

The down side was that I was soon feeling a little bit homesick. Even one night in the hotel felt like too long spent away from my family, and it seemed like such a big distance. I wanted to be with Karen and the kids, and be a husband and father. I quickly worked out that if we were not on a double-session I could get my skates on, wolf some lunch down and be back in Southampton to pick the kids up from school. It was a two-and-a-half hour journey and it became my daily commute. I spent a lot of time in the car.

* * *

The magic of football had worn thin long before this point. Most professional footballers will recognise the transformation from the game you learn to love as a child, kicking a ball around in the playground without a care, to the ruthless and competitive world where almost the only thing of any importance is that you win.

The quality of your work has repercussions for your family, your teammates, your club and the fans. There is a lot at stake and pressure builds up. There was not a stage in my career when I ever felt able to sit back and take anything for granted.

On a week-to-week basis, I felt as if I had to impress against a backdrop of uncertainty. There were low points, such as my disciplinary problems and the times when new managers came in and started signing players for my position.

I conditioned myself not to become too carried away with a good game or a victory and not too low after a defeat. I tended to be hard on myself. I always knew if I was having a bad game and I was the sort to beat myself up. I didn't need other people telling me. I'd be aware of it already.

Don't get me wrong, I enjoyed my career and I am grateful for it, but I was always mindful that it was a job and I was providing for my family. I had to stay in the team, and win a new contract. Your perspective changes over time. I never forgot it was a privilege to be a player but it was always more serious than that.

* * *

I made 15 appearances in all for Nottingham Forest, all of them at left-back. Unfortunately, we did not make the anticipated end-of-season push for promotion but my time there did provide me with one very fond memory. I knew when I signed they were in the same division as Portsmouth, and one of the first things I did was to scan the fixtures, with my eyes quickly drawn to a date at Fratton Park in early April.

That was one I was looking forward to if I was still at the club and it turned out that I was, because I extended the initial loan at the City Ground by another month, and then another.

I had never played a competitive senior game against Pompey. They had been relegated a few months before I made my first team debut and did not return until 2003, when I was about to retire. By a random twist, Portsmouth's 15-year absence from the top flight of English football coincided almost precisely with my senior career.

I did play against them in the reserves and was in the team when we won 5–1 at Fratton Park in a testimonial game for Alan Knight, their legendary goalkeeper. There was very little good spirit to that occasion. It was a big crowd and a hostile reception for us. We didn't approach it as a friendly, and we won convincingly. The referee was very generous to award them a penalty and allow them to score a goal.

We were drawn against them in the third round of the FA Cup in 1995–96, which generated a real buzz. It was the first derby for more than eight years and, for weeks between the draw and the match at The Dell, it was the only thing supporters wanted to talk about.

I was devastated when I found out I wasn't selected. Dave Merrington was the manager at the time and he pulled me aside to explain his decision. He thought he needed cool heads out there, because of what was at stake and said he could not run the risk with my temperament in a game like this.

Simon Charlton played instead of me at left-back and we won easily. I was part of the squad and enjoyed the victory but it was not quite the same as it would have been had I been out there in a Saints shirt. That would have been an amazing experience for me personally.

When we turned up at Fratton Park with Forest, the home fans were yelling abuse at me from the moment I stepped from the coach. They did not see me as a Forest player that night. I could have been wearing any kit. Every time the ball went out and I went to pick it up there were people on their feet screaming 'scummer', the particular insult Pompey fans like to reserve for people from Southampton.

As far as those supporters were concerned, I was a Saints player. I relished the animosity. It was only a shame I couldn't be playing in a Saints shirt. Although, unbeknown to them, I was in a Saints shirt. I dug out one of my old Southampton training vests with a badge on the chest and wore it underneath my Forest shirt. We won 2–0 and I savoured the win and the clean sheet and made the most of the celebrations.

Dave Beasant, another former Saints player, was in goal for us. I made a beeline for him at the end. We both lingered on the pitch, milking the applause from the away fans, which didn't go down well with the locals. We were still punching the air as we came off. Some of the home fans tried to swing at us as we went down the steps and down the tunnel on our way back to the changing rooms. Dave later signed for Pompey and maybe they forgave him but he was firmly in the enemy camp at this time.

Karen had been to watch the game, and we drove home down the M27, giving Dave a lift back to a hotel in Fareham where he had left his car. Only when we were back at training in Nottingham did we realise a group of irate Portsmouth supporters had tried to force their way onto the Forest team bus, shouting, 'Where the hell is Benali?'

* * *

My three months on loan were soon up. Nottingham Forest had the option to make the loan deal permanent. They were pushing for the play-offs but were losing money at the time and so it was difficult for them to make any commitment. David Platt told the media he would like to keep me but there was 'as much chance of signing Luis Figo', the Portugal international who was playing for Real Madrid and recognised as one of the best footballers in the world. So, not much chance then. I can't recall another time when I was compared to Figo.

A few weeks earlier, Glenn Hoddle had left Southampton to become manager of Tottenham. He had been with Saints for 14 months and John Gorman went with him. It was no surprise. I never felt he was in it for the long term. That is not to say his heart wasn't in it. He wanted to do well but I always had a feeling that if the Spurs job came up he would go, given his relationship and history with the club. I watched the move unfold from afar. I could understand his decision. If that had been me and Southampton I would have done the same.

I can't say I was too unhappy to be heading back. I had one more year remaining on my contract. I wanted a chance to impress the next manager and this was an emotional time because we were playing out the last few games at The Dell.

Stuart Gray took over as caretaker manager for the rest of the season and we did well under him. I came off the bench in three of the last four games in the season, including the win against Arsenal, the last competitive game at The Dell. It was not a bad way to bid farewell to the old ground, and that flurry of positive results was enough to earn Stuart the job on a full-time basis.

Stuart was a fabulous coach and a lovely guy. I was delighted for him to get the chance and from a personal perspective it was encouraging. Stuart made it clear he wanted me back, he made me feel wanted again. It was fabulous to be back at Southampton and to be part of the move into the new stadium at St Mary's. It was an exciting time.

* * *

There had been talk of building a new stadium for years. It was badly needed if the club was going to move forwards. We had been battling against the odds at The Dell because of its limited capacity. We had seen football changing and improvements to the stadiums where we played. First there was the move to all-seater grounds, then came the growth of the corporate sector.

When Rupert Lowe became chairman he drove through the move to St Mary's. A lot of supporters disliked Rupert. He didn't have a football background and was different to your typical football man. He was part of the change in direction for football.

Personally, I had no issues with him. He was always good to me and I found him straightforward and honest. I was club captain and, when there was an off-pitch issue I had to take to the board, his door was open. I had a good working relationship with him. I did employ an agent for one contract, but mostly I would deal with my own negotiations, which meant sitting and speaking directly with the manager or, in the latter years, with Rupert.

The first point of discussion would always be to find out if there was a new deal on the table. I was never threatening to run down my contract or strengthen my position by pretending I was looking to move elsewhere. Everybody knew how I felt. If the club was prepared to offer me a new deal, great. Then, what are the terms? What's the length of contract? What's the salary? I can never remember having a disagreement. Maybe that was to my detriment. Maybe that was reflected in my salary but I was always happy with what I was earning, happy doing what I was doing at Southampton and didn't feel like I needed an agent.

The transition to St Mary's however, was not easy because all those little things we used to our advantage at The Dell were gone. The visiting teams had lovely new dressing rooms and supporters were a long way from the pitch. It seemed huge. There was a big wide tunnel, quite a contrast to the old staircase. On the pitch, it was not so easy to create the same levels of intensity and build pressure on the opposition. The atmosphere just wasn't the same.

So as wonderful as it was to be moving to a state-of-the-art stadium, it lacked something. It was exciting and we all knew we needed to do it, but it was so unfamiliar. The weirdest thing was walking in through the glass doors and finding everything branded as Southampton Football Club, yet finding it felt alien. Beyond the colours and logos, it could have been any ground, anywhere in the world. It never felt like our home, certainly not in those early days. A few of us missed The Dell more than others because it was all we'd ever known. Creating a relationship with the new stadium was difficult and that was reflected in the results.

Weeks went by at the start of the new season without a home win and it became a concern, to the extent where some people thought there was a curse on the land and the club bizarrely arranged for a pagan witch to come in and perform some sort of ceremony to banish it. I don't know if it was a PR stunt or if someone higher up at the club actually thought the ground was cursed.

We didn't win a home game until the end of November by which time Stuart had been sacked and replaced by Gordon Strachan. I felt for Stuart and sad that I wasn't able as part of the squad to make things better for him. He played a big part in me coming back to the club after my three months on loan at Nottingham Forest and I would have loved to see him flourish as a manager at Southampton.

Instead, we were back into the unknown with another manager coming in, back to square one. What would he think of me as a player? Could I prove myself all over again? Nothing new there. We had a gathering at the training ground, where Gordon addressed us all, his first collective talk with all the players and staff in the canteen, which then doubled up as the meeting room where we would watch video clips and have team talks.

He said he realised it would take time for us to get to know each other but that he knew a few things already and there were one or two players he could remember playing against. 'How could I forget Franny

Benali,' he said. 'Franny clattered me so hard I was left with bruises the length of my back for weeks.'

This was his first speech since taking the job. I sank deeper into my chair thinking this wasn't a great way to start, with the new manager recalling the day I kicked lumps out of him. Gordon was a great footballer and I'd actually kicked him many times but I instantly knew the occasion he was referring to. He was at Leeds and I remembered it quite clearly because he really was not happy at all. The fiery side of his nature came out that day and he let me know exactly what he thought about the challenge.

But there was no reason for me to be concerned. Gordon has a great sense of humour and he was fantastic for me because he saw the value of having senior players around, such as myself, Matt Le Tissier and Jason Dodd. We had knowledge and experience of Southampton and he was astute enough to use that. He consulted us, especially in the early days and encouraged our input. He would call the three of us into meetings and talk about a few things. Doddsy continued to play regularly for Gordon in 2001–02 but Matt had been struggling with muscle injuries for months. His body simply could not stand up to the rigours of professional football any longer. He retired in the summer of 2002, while I agreed to sign for one more year.

This was going to be my last playing contract at Southampton. Gordon was open and honest about that and I signed on the understanding that I would be playing on a very occasional basis, if at all. I had no alternative plan going into the season. I suppose I was trying to work out what I might do next. I turned over the same old dilemma in my mind: I was not prepared to uproot Karen and the kids for the sake of a year or two playing at a lower level at that stage of my career and I did not want to commute, even if it was somewhere closer than Nottingham. I did not regret my three months at Forest but I did not want to go down that route again. I dismissed the idea of going out on loan again or looking for a transfer. I chose to stay at Saints.

I soon got my head around the idea that I would not be starting games so often but I still thought, 'It would be great to be on the bench.' Gordon usually announced the team on the day before the game at a meeting in the canteen at Staplewood. Then we would go out run through a little bit of shape and set-pieces. We didn't know the subs until we reported to the stadium on match day. I started to find I wasn't even being named among the five substitutes, as it was at the time. I tried to stay positive and Gordon made sure I felt valued. He sought my counsel at times and might ask me to join the squad on an away trip, even though I wasn't going to be involved.

My complete understanding and appreciation of the situation did not make it any easier. It did not suppress my urge to want to play, or contribute more to the team effort. Those little knocks can build up. It is a horrible feeling when you long for something and it doesn't happen.

My role had changed from having an impact as a player on the pitch to trying to bring some value to training and around the dressing room by trying to motivate and encourage and offer advice here and there, chatting to one or two players.

I started to work regularly with Steve Wigley, who had joined the Southampton coaching staff from Forest and was mostly looking after the younger players. I tried to pass on my advice and knowledge within the sessions and I tried to motivate myself in training by thinking there was always a chance I might be needed.

Wayne Bridge was now our first choice left-back, making excellent progress and maturing into a terrific footballer. Saints fans voted him their Player of the Year in 2000–01. He broke into the England squad and went to the World Cup finals in 2002. Moreover, from my point of view, he never seemed to be injured – or even tired.

When he first broke in, we played together on the left side, him on the wing and me at full-back, but once Glenn Hoddle moved me aside, Bridgey really seized his chance at left-back. I am pleased in many ways that it was someone like him who finally displaced me. He was a local boy coming through the ranks and someone I genuinely liked a lot.

He played 113 consecutive league games for Southampton without missing a single minute. For two whole seasons he was ever-present. This stood as a Premier League record for an outfield player until Frank Lampard passed it. It felt like a lifetime for me at that stage in my career. All I wanted to do was make a contribution. His record-breaking run started in March 2000 and it ended when he damaged a calf muscle during a game against Liverpool in January 2003.

I didn't wait too long before I knocked on Gordon Strachan's door. I knew Bridgey was going to be out for a few weeks and we had done a few training sessions where I could see he was considering me. I was the only other specialist left-back in the squad, although he could move others like Danny Higginbotham, Rory Delap or Chris Marsden in there.

It must have been prominent in Gordon's mind that it was a long time since I had played – only six substitute appearances in nearly two years since my return from Nottingham Forest, and 16 months since the most recent of them. I had not played a single minute in the first team since Stuart Gray was sacked.

I had been training and trying to stay as sharp as I could. We worked hard in training under Gordon. We were the fittest squad I'd known at any stage in my career. I'd been playing in the reserves, although that is never the same. I didn't have the right level of match fitness. Even so, I wanted to see Gordon face-to-face and let him know I was ready to play and wouldn't let him down.

I don't know if that helped him make the decision, but I was back in the team for the FA Cup fourth round tie at home against Millwall. Just to get back out there was wonderful and was something I'd missed for so long, watching from the touchlines, wanting to be playing and training as hard as I could. It was like making my debut all over again, at the age of 34.

Although my game was rusty, it was great to be on that stage with something at stake. I made a sliding goal line clearance to stop Millwall taking an early lead through Steve Claridge, and made an important block in the penalty area. As a defender you hardly ever get recognition but I knew my efforts had gone a long way to the final outcome. I even played a small part in the build-up to our equaliser, scored in the last minute by Kevin Davies, who, like myself, had been on the fringes of the team. It was nice for us to feel like we were helping the cause.

I kept my place in the team for games against Sunderland and Manchester United in the Premier League, and the FA Cup replay at Millwall, when Matt Oakley scored twice and we won in extra time.

Unfortunately I picked up a calf injury in the replay at Millwall, not bad enough to force me off, but I had to go and have quite a lot of blood drained away from the muscle. Maybe those four games in 10 days, including extra time, had taken their toll after so long out of competitive action. Danny Higginbotham took over at left-back as we overcame Norwich in the FA Cup fifth round, and Bridgey was back for Wolverhampton Wanderers in the quarter-finals.

There was a positive vibe inside the club. Gordon had created an exciting team. We were fit and we played with real energy and intensity. We had a good balance of characters, quality players, a blend of youth and experience and our confidence was growing. In the FA Cup, the draw had been kind and a route to the final opened up. After Wolves, we beat Watford in a semi-final at Villa Park. Saints were back in the FA Cup Final for the first time since 1976.

Arsenal, the holders, were our opponents, at the Millennium Stadium in Cardiff because Wembley was being rebuilt. There was a huge buzz around the city and it seemed to be all people were talking about.

It was a great way for me to end my career. The FA Cup was special for anyone of my generation who watched Lawrie's Southampton team win it. The competition had always been a big thing for me. I was only sorry Matt Le Tissier wasn't still with us. We used to talk about winning the FA Cup and every year we tried without ever making it further than the quarter-finals.

But I know he would not have enjoyed Gordon's training regime. When we met for preseason just a few weeks after Matt's retirement in 2002, we went to St Andrews in Scotland. Gordon had us running in the sand dunes to build our stamina levels. It was horrendous, one of the hardest preseasons I had known. I was exhausted and I called Matt to tell him what we were doing – from the student accommodation where we were staying. It seemed that someone at the club decided we might benefit from a change of policy and we did not stay in a hotel with the luxuries we usually enjoyed when travelling away. Matt laughed down the phone and told me retirement didn't sound too bad after all. One thing he didn't miss was the preseason. Still, it was weird not having him around. I had lost someone who had always been with me, and Southampton could no longer call upon the club's greatest player. Then, suddenly, despite his absence, we make it all the way to the FA Cup Final.

I knew I wasn't going to be starting against Arsenal but I was grateful to be part of the larger squad as we set off to Cardiff. We were measured up for our Cup Final suits by Ted Baker. I was already a friend of Ray Kelvin, the founder of Ted, and our families have become close over the years. We stayed in a plush hotel on the water on the eve of the game, and I was able to savour the journey to the stadium. I walked out onto the pitch with the rest of the players, soaking up the atmosphere and waved to my family in the stands. It was mind-blowing to see the mass of yellow and blue, our away colours.

The roof was closed for the first time in an FA Cup Final and the noise sent a tingle down my spine. Hairs stood up on the back of my neck. Deep down in my heart I clung to the hope I might be on the bench. How I would have loved to be getting changed and pulling on my boots. What a finish that would have been. But it wasn't the case.

Gordon's big selection decision on the day was to start with Chris Baird ahead of Fabrice Fernandes.

Chris was 21 and making only his second start in a senior game. Ten days earlier, we had played Arsenal away in the Premier League and lost 6–1. I was there at Highbury and Gordon went ballistic about Fabrice's performance. I'm certain that cost him his place in the final and it must have been tough to swallow.

There's always an element missing if you're not involved in the team. I moved towards my seat alongside the bench as they were starting to play the national anthem and all I could think of was being out there playing. It was a strange mix of emotions. I knew there would not be another playing contract on the table at Southampton but, as this season was nearing its end, they were kind enough to offer me a coaching role. Whatever happened, this was the last game I would experience as a Saints player.

Robert Pires scored for Arsenal in the first half and they kept us at arm's length for the rest of the game. They were an exceptional side under Arsène Wenger. The following season, they went on to win the Premier League title without losing a game, an incredible achievement. We tried but we couldn't find a way back in Cardiff. It would have been nice to see one of the boys score just to witness the explosion of joy from of our supporters. We had been on a journey together and we all believed we could win, so to stand out on the pitch after a 1–0 defeat and watch Arsenal lift the trophy was quite sad.

There always has to be a loser in a Cup Final. The dressing room was silent. Most people were thinking what could have been. We had come so close to doing something very special and we walked back in as runners-up. So near yet so far.

Gordon spoke to the group and said, 'You have all been incredible and if you find yourselves in this position again, remember what this feeling is like, and do everything you can to make sure you're on the other side of it.'

Players started moving around the dressing room, hitting the showers. One or two conversations got going. I sat at my peg near Michael Svensson and Danny Higginbotham. Danny looked at me, offered his medal and said, 'Franny you've been here for your entire career, you deserve this more than I do, I'd like you to have it.'

I choked up. I knew he meant it. Danny was a joker, but this was genuine and he was willing to give away his medal. I've laughed about it since and said it might have been different if we'd won the Cup. Would he have been giving away his winner's medal? But the gesture was true and it made me feel very emotional.

I thanked him but I couldn't accept it. That was his medal. He played his part in the Cup run and he deserved to keep it. Fortunately, the club were able to get hold of a few extra medals and gave them to those players who made the odd appearance on the way to the final like Kevin Davies, Jason Dodd and myself, which was a nice touch.

My playing career was at an end, nearly 15 years after my debut against Derby. I had made 389 appearances for Saints, plus 15 for Nottingham Forest. The last of them in the FA Cup replay, away at Millwall on 5 February 2003.

There was, however, a postscript. It came in the Ted Bates Trophy, a friendly match set up to honour a man who devoted his life to Southampton FC. Ted served as player, manager, director and club president before he died in November 2003, six months after our FA Cup final defeat, at the age of 85. We organised a game against Bayern Munich, who sent a strong team including Michael Ballack and Owen Hargreaves. It ended in a 1–1 draw.

I was on the coaching staff and Gordon Strachan said he would like me to have a run out in this game, one final appearance in a Saints shirt to say farewell and thank you to the supporters, and vice-versa.

I've never been one to swap shirts. I have a Juventus shirt from a preseason trip to Italy where we played them in a tournament, but my collection of shirts consists mostly of my Southampton tops from different eras. I tried to keep one from every season. I have the one I wore on my debut, the old Hummel kit sponsored by Draper Tools. I wore a few of my old Saints shirts when I ran a garden marathon for charity on a treadmill during the coronavirus lockdown in 2020.

Swapping shirts wasn't really the done thing in my time. The kit was washed and worn again but Ballack's shirt became a prime target that night for lots of the lads. They went chasing after him after the final whistle. I left them to it. I was drifting around the pitch, trying to take in the occasion. The supporters were singing my name and I was emotional because I knew it would be for the last time. I was close to tears when one of the younger Bayern players came over and asked me to exchange shirts, which I did.

I didn't know who he was, but he went on to have a brilliant career and I became the proud owner of a Bastian Schweinsteiger shirt. It is enormous – we wore them baggy in those days. When he won the World Cup with Germany in 2014 and went on to captain that formidable national team, it seemed like a cool piece of memorabilia to have.

7

AN AFTER LIFE

'Ever since I was a little boy, the first question I get asked when I'm at a Saints game is what it is like having a dad who was a professional footballer. The truth is, I don't really remember the football as I was very young, only just leaving primary school when Dad retired, and he didn't play a lot during the seasons before that as Wayne Bridge was bursting through.

Most of the images I have of him playing football are from watching old clips online, but I was an adult when I watched him take on his three ultra-endurance challenges. I saw the hours of intense training and what it did to him. I saw him getting up at four or five in the morning to get in the pool, constantly pushing his body to new extremes.

How he did all that, I will never know. On the second challenge, I ran for 20 miles with him and could barely walk afterwards, but Dad had a quick stop for lunch and then hopped on his bike and cycled for 100 miles. He made it look effortless and smiled throughout. I think it was only when he started to show some of the pain he was in that everyone realised the sheer fatigue he was causing himself.

So what is it like having a footballer for a dad? I don't know, I don't really remember the football. But having my dad for a dad? I wouldn't change it for the world.'

Luke Benali, Franny's son

One day you're a footballer and the next day you're not. The process is abrupt, whatever the circumstances, and it is hard.

I can see why so many people find the transition to be such a struggle. Overnight you lose the sense of camaraderie and an element of identity. You lose the buzz from stepping out in front of a crowd and doing something you love.

The trade off is that you get a little more flexibility. You can go out and meet friends at the weekend, and not worry about eating the odd takeaway or whether you're getting the right amount of sleep. You don't have to spend Christmas Day in a hotel and you can book a family holiday at Easter if that's what you want to do.

Unless, of course, you decide to go straight into coaching. My career had shifted towards coaching during the years under Gordon Strachan. It seemed like a natural step. I had been club captain for years and I was engaged in the community side of the club and, towards the end of my playing days, I realised part of my role was to encourage others, offer advice and set an example.

I accepted the offer of a coaching role at Southampton and moved out of the first team dressing room at the training ground and into the coaches' room next door. I worked predominantly with Steve Wigley, who was coaching the young professionals not in the first team squad. I would also take charge of the Under-12s in the academy, which involved training twice a week in the evenings and a game at the weekend, usually on a Sunday.

Financially it was a considerable change. I wasn't a huge earner from a player's perspective but I dropped from a first team player's salary – and training a few hours each day – to a junior coach's salary and I was working many times harder. This was a big culture shock. As much as I enjoyed it, I found it difficult to adjust to the hours, and a lot of my family time just vanished.

Typically, I would train Monday to Friday, mornings and some afternoons, take training with the Under-12s on two evenings, and be with the reserve team at a game on another night in midweek. If the first team was at home at the weekend, I would work with the young pros on a Saturday morning before going straight to St Mary's for the match.

I would be back home early in the evening then be up at the crack of dawn on a Sunday morning, often travelling to London with the Under-12s, then back home in the evening before starting a new week on Monday morning. It was absolutely full on. I will forever be grateful for my lifestyle as a player because it gave me the time to be with my family and see the children grow up.

As the months went by I soon realised coaching wasn't for me. I didn't even make it to the end of the season in the role. I felt a little bit guilty because so many people at the club had tried to help me to embrace the transition.

Wigs, in particular, had been very supportive. I had worked under him as a player, he was a fantastic coach and we always had a great relationship. He knew I was missing my family time and would sometimes tell me to get off early and see the kids, but it wasn't a difficult decision for me when I looked ahead and tried to envisage the next 5, 10 or 15 years.

I could not see myself climbing the coaching ladder at Southampton. The likelihood of ever getting a chance to be manager of the club was highly unlikely – in the past coaches had been promoted from within to take the top job and it had not worked out particularly well. I certainly had no desire to trek around the country earning my stripes as a manager in the hope of coming back to Saints one day.

I had already gone into partnership with my father-in-law in the building and property trade, and I decided to throw my energy into that. I branched out once or twice during my playing days because I realised football was not a career that would last forever. I invested in Kuti's, a Bangladeshi restaurant in the city centre in the '90s, which I enjoyed, and there were a couple of other projects along the way, too.

Footballers are always getting into conversations about the future, when they're around a table over a meal or while travelling on the long coach journeys to and from the games. What exactly are you going to do next? What can you do?

Some people had very definite plans. Ian Andrews, who was a goalkeeper at Southampton, was always set on the idea of going into physiotherapy and he would carry huge text books onto the coach when we were going to away games. Ian would have his nose in a book, studying and working towards his qualifications and, when his playing career finished, he did go on to become a successful physio, so it was worth the effort and dedication.

That day comes for everyone. Our generation, on the whole, didn't earn enough money to retire and do nothing.

* * *

Harry Redknapp was manager of Southampton when I volunteered to make a comeback, at the age of 36.

I had reverted from being a player and coach back to a full-time Saints supporter and I could not help feeling angry and frustrated as I watched the team slide towards relegation. I knew how close we had been to the drop on quite a few occasions when I was playing, and I knew how we went about getting out of trouble. Unfortunately, a number of the players I was watching on a regular basis did not appear to have the same care and passion for the club.

Ultimately, the worst happened in the 2004–05 season. Relegation. Something I'd spent my entire career fighting to avoid, along with so many others. I'm not saying for one second the reason we went down was because the old guard was no longer there. There were good people still in the dressing room such as Claus Lundekvam, Jason Dodd and Matt Oakley. I know how much it meant to them, but there were probably not enough players with the same desire.

I was very nearly shouting in frustration in some games when I watched Olivier Bernard, on loan from Newcastle and playing in my position at left-back, displaying what I saw as such a lack of desire or will to win or get a result, or even care. From where I was sitting, he didn't seem to give a damn about what happened to the club because he would just be moving on or going back to his club. I wanted to go and kick some of them up the backside.

Something was missing, something wasn't right. The players didn't seem to have the same personalities and the same bond. Harry had come in as manager and there was lots of drama about that because he had come from Portsmouth. A few of the comments he made were not very positive. He made it sound as though he was coming into a sinking ship.

Once Saints were in the Championship, the standard wasn't as high as in the Premier League and I thought it might be a level where I could still play if I got my fitness back. I thought my experience could also help in the dressing room. I'm sure there was an element of me just wanting to play football again because I missed it but mostly I wanted to help. I thought I would at least ask the question. I knew Kevin Bond, who was on Harry's coaching staff, so I gave Kevin a call and that conversation led to an invitation to the training ground to have a chat with Harry.

I knew it sounded odd but I told him I'd be willing to come in and train and see how it went, just to see if there was a possibility of coming back. I wasn't after a big contract and I would have signed on a pay-as-you-play deal. Harry seemed to welcome the idea. He told me to come in, train and see how things went. It was preseason and I went in for a few weeks. I knew there was a lot of work to be done on my fitness. I played in a friendly against Eastleigh and did OK, playing at left-back. Matt Le Tissier made an appearance for Eastleigh as a late substitute.

It didn't come to anything though. Whenever I asked Harry, he would always say something like he'd speak to the chairman, or the chairman was struggling to 'make it happen'. I don't think there was ever any real passion for the idea from him. Sometimes I question whether Harry and Rupert Lowe ever had a proper conversation on the subject.

Maybe he thought it would look like too much of a desperate measure for a former player to come out of retirement and back into the fold. It might not have looked good from his perspective and it didn't happen. I would have preferred it if he'd said, 'Sorry Franny but I can't do this.'

* * *

Watching Southampton struggle from the outside was not a pleasant experience at all. Matt Le Tissier and I remained close. We would meet regularly and often talked, and one of the main areas of debate at this time was the dismal state of the club we both loved. We agreed it needed a boost to lift it back to where it once was and, when Harry was sacked in December 2005 and the search for another manager began, we offered to help.

What had started out as a light-hearted conversation over dinner quite quickly developed into something more serious and reached the point where we approached the club to pitch the idea of going in as the new management team.

Sir Clive Woodward, the head coach who masterminded England's Rugby World Cup win in 2003, had been appointed as the club's performance director, and we went to meet him at his apartment in Southampton.

We discussed our proposal but it didn't go any further. It was one meeting and, on reflection, maybe a good thing it didn't happen. Neither of us had any formal qualifications or experience of managing a team. We would have given it our best shot but it could easily have tarnished our relationship with the club and the supporters if we had gone in and things had gone badly.

Sir Clive came in for a lot of criticism during his short time at Southampton, as did Rupert Lowe for making the appointment. It was very uncommon for anyone to cross from rugby to football but I had seen him speak at a dinner at St Mary's Stadium and was intrigued by innovations he might be able to bring to the club.

He had achieved so much in rugby and I would have loved to be a player and hear some of his ideas and methods relating to how he thought we could improve, whether something out of the ordinary or just a simple change.

I was also quite excited to find out if he could convert what he had done in rugby to football. But there were such a lot of internal battles going on at Southampton at the time. Sir Clive clashed with Harry and his coaching team. There were ownership disputes and power struggles. It probably wasn't the right environment for him. People were pulling the club in different directions and personalities were not getting along. None of this was good for the club. In fact, there must have been a hell of a lot going wrong.

During my playing career, we escaped relegation so routinely that I thought we would never go down. Now, here they were, in the Championship and still dropping. They slipped into League One in 2009. It was shocking to see the club plunge to such depths. They had not been in the third tier in my lifetime. I went along and tried to offer support and I did some hospitality work in the suites at St Mary's but it was a tough watch.

* * *

When I did pull my boots on again in a competitive sense it was at the age of 37 to play for Eastleigh, who were in the sixth tier of English football, then called the Conference South. I'd been out of the game for two years and it was at least partly a financial move as I tried to pick up another income stream. Eastleigh were ambitious and they were paying good money for part-time players on the local non-league scene.

The only dilemma was interest from Salisbury City, when they heard I was considering a return to football. The big draw at Salisbury was the manager, Nick Holmes, who was one of Southampton's FA Cup heroes of 1976 and a senior pro when I was starting out. On Nick's staff, as a player-coach was Tommy Widdrington, who had been with me for many years at Saints.

I went to join them for a few training sessions and they had a good set-up but I made the decision to sign for Eastleigh, mainly because it was closer. It was on my doorstep. Paul Doswell was manager at the time, and he later stepped up to be director of football and Jason Dodd took over. Doddsy had signed with me as a player at the start of the season but picked up an ankle injury and it forced him to retire. He was another familiar face from my time at Saints, a fellow full-back who had had a long and excellent career.

The football was competitive and a good standard and I played predominantly as a left-back. I found it difficult training only a couple of nights a week. Throughout my professional career, I always felt as if I had to immerse myself to reach my best. I wasn't able to switch it on and off like some players. I had to train hard and be fully committed if I was going to play well on a Saturday. I wasn't at peak fitness as we trained only a couple of nights a week, and my age might have been catching up with me.

We played Salisbury in the third qualifying round of the FA Cup, although I missed the game through suspension. Some things didn't change. The most challenging part was a simmering frustration, which was nothing to do with the ability of my teammates or the opposition. There were lots of good players, but I had a real problem with the officials. I thought I had mellowed a bit with age but I allowed the refereeing to get into my head in a negative way. I had always had my run-ins with officials over the years at Saints but here I was again, getting myself worked up because I felt the standard wasn't high enough. I really struggled with that.

Nick and Tommy's Salisbury side knocked us out of the FA Cup, which was a shame. A nice little run in that competition is important to the clubs at that level. Salisbury went on to reach the second round proper, where they took Nottingham Forest to a replay at the City Ground.

I made 22 appearances for Eastleigh. No goals – so nothing had changed there either. I picked up an injury towards the end of the season when I hurt my arm colliding in training with one of my teammates. It was the forearm with the steel plate inserted. I was in such excruciating pain I thought I must have broken it again. I had a cast fitted to immobilise it, which meant I missed the last run of games.

I knew then I could not commit to another season. I had enjoyed my year with Eastleigh, getting to know the people there, but even before I had a chance to tell them how I felt about another season, they told me they couldn't afford to keep me on. And that was that.

* * *

Our property company was struggling in the wake of the global recession and, as a result of our financial position, we were considering the idea of selling or renting out our home.

It was a tough decision because Karen and I had designed 'Springwood' ourselves with the help of an architect. It was a dream home and the place where our children Luke and Kenzie had started to grow up. We had five bedrooms and an indoor swimming pool, a cinema room, stables, quite a lot of land and beautiful unspoiled views over Forestry Commission land.

It was in the same lane as Karen's parents, Bill and Eileen, in the Chilworth area of the city. We had been living there for a few years when we had to face up to the big decision of whether we should sell it or rent it out and move into something smaller and more cost effective. This was all happening in 2009, at a time when Markus Liebherr became the new owner of Southampton FC and installed Nicola Cortese as chairman, responsible for the day-to-day running of the club.

Through my contacts at the club, I found out that Cortese was looking to rent a property in the city for himself and his family. It struck me as the perfect solution. It would help with our finances and we had such a close connection to the club that we trusted them implicitly to always do the right thing. I thought it was a no-brainer. I told Karen there wouldn't be any problems with this. Famous last words.

When we first met Nicola Cortese he seemed like a most charming man. He could not have been more pleasant. He viewed the property with his wife and came back to say they would like to rent it. We had the house valued by an independent company and told him the figures we were looking for.

This, he said, was more than the club would allow him for a monthly budget but he suggested I came back to the club and did some hospitality work in a paid role in order to make up for what would be a shortfall in rent.

This wasn't entirely fair. I would be going in and working for part of the rent but I enjoyed working at the club. I had done some hospitality work in the past and was more than happy to go back and get involved again.

We agreed for me to go in and work at home games and I had a tenancy agreement drawn up along with a detailed inventory because I wanted to do it right. It was a long and detailed document. Thank goodness I didn't cut any corners because we later had it to fall back on.

Initially, I had the tenancy agreement drawn up in Cortese's name and sent it off to be signed. It came straight back and he insisted it should be drawn up in the name of the football club. I didn't think too much about this at the time, did as he requested, and changed it to say the football club but this would become a source of great heartache.

Within a few weeks of him moving into the house, the whole situation erupted and I started to become aware of things going on at the property. Cortese was making changes at the house and was using staff from the club to do the work. Someone at the club tipped me off about what was going on. He was redecorating, pulling carpets up and putting new flooring down.

We weren't far away because we had moved in with my in-laws, Bill and Eileen, who lived in the same lane. One day, we received some of the Cortese family's mail by accident, so Karen walked down the lane to deliver it. There, she noticed our carpets rolled up and stacked outside, and there were loads of paint cans.

I would expect any tenant to make the place more personal. To put up a few pictures, maybe, but I wasn't prepared for him to go in and start making drastic changes without even asking us. I thought it lacked respect, as well as going against the tenancy agreement. I sought a meeting with him. I went to see him at St Mary's, and sat down with him in his office where he was talking at great length about his new desk, a big beautiful wooden desk, which had just been shipped over from Italy at goodness knows what cost to the club.

He pointed at the desk and said: 'What do you think of this?' I said it was lovely. And it was. Then he pointed out something. He was clearly insinuating there was an imperfection of some kind. I couldn't see anything. He said: 'This is going back. This is not good enough. It must be changed.'

I just raised my eyebrows. I couldn't see anything wrong with it but that wasn't really my business. I was there to talk about my property and to tell him that I really didn't like the way he was making so many changes in the house without seeking permission, especially as they were so unnecessary.

He could have promised to put everything back the way it had been at the end of the agreement and I would probably have accepted that, but instead he started telling me how he was planning to make other changes to some of the en-suite bathrooms.

This lack of respect really annoyed me. I said, 'Let me stop you there, you're not making any more changes at the property. From what I've heard, you've made enough changes already and haven't had the decency to ask me about them first.'

He flipped, changed instantly and started getting very worked up. He flew into a rage. All of a sudden I saw a completely different side to him. I said, 'If anyone should be getting worked up here, it's me, not you.' I told him I didn't want to see any more changes and that he had to adhere to the agreement we had in place.

From this point on, he would not answer my calls or respond to my emails or messages. If I tried to contact him, I would have to speak to a member of staff at the club, people I'd known for decades, since the start of my time at Southampton. I could understand the predicament they were in as employees and the pressure they were under with the way he ran the club. I could see what was going on.

Things got worse when I received correspondence from Southampton telling me not to come in for my hospitality work. This had been part of the original agreement to offset the shortfall in rent and if I didn't come in I was going to lose income. I was concerned I could be breaching the agreement by failing to do my hospitality work.

I turned up at the next game and made my way towards the suite where I usually worked. One of the members of staff stopped me outside. She told me the chairman had given orders that I wasn't allowed into the club and would have to be escorted from the premises.

I didn't want to cause a scene outside the suite by demanding to see the chairman or insisting to do my job in accordance with our agreement. At the same time, I wasn't prepared to back down when I had done nothing wrong. I said I didn't want to miss the game and I wasn't going to leave. I made my way up towards one of the executive boxes and watched the game from there.

Next came a letter from Southampton to say that because of my stance on the property I would not be welcome inside the stadium. I couldn't believe it. I now felt excluded from the football club, banned to all intents and purpose and all because I had questioned Cortese and told him I did not want him to make any more changes to my own home.

This was his style. I've heard the stories about the way he behaved inside the club, how he treated people. Allegedly, he even had his own personal toilet installed and no one else was allowed to use it.

As chairman of Southampton, he could behave the way he did because of the position he held. If he didn't get his way he would throw an even bigger strop. He was a complete coward from what I could tell, a bully who was making people's lives an absolute misery at the club. I had never met anyone like him in my life. I hope I never meet anyone like him again. He was an absolute disgrace in my opinion and I wasn't prepared to stand for it.

Our dispute turned nasty and it came to consume our family. We felt as if there was no other option than to take legal advice. I wanted him out of the house and served him with notice on the tenancy. He vacated the property but not before the end of the term.

When he eventually left, we pursued a claim for my lost income at the club and for damages caused at the house. But, very soon, we had racked up more than £10,000 in legal fees and there was no end in sight. It could have dragged on for years and we couldn't afford to keep paying it. He may well have been stringing it out in the hope that we would run out of money and drop the case.

Our solicitors agreed to take it up on a no-win-no-fee basis. They knew what a strong case we had. Ever since he had flipped on me during that meeting in his office, I had taken care to keep a detailed paper trail to document every communication. At the start of the legal proceedings, both Karen and I turned up carrying these enormous files.

Many months later, there was a pre-trial hearing in Winchester for the judge to make one last attempt to sort it out before it went into court. There were representatives from the football club but Cortese didn't turn up. I don't know how that went down in the eyes of the judge.

This was the stage in proceedings when I discovered the overall legal fees. I nearly fell off my chair when I found out. Ultimately, these legal costs would have to be paid by Southampton FC and it was a complete, unnecessary waste of the club's money.

A court date was set and I had reached the point where I was looking forward to having this out in a courtroom but a few days before the case was due, our solicitors called us to say the dispute was settled. It was May 2013, and the very same day Sir Alex Ferguson revealed he would step down as the manager of Manchester United at the end of the season.

We had spent hours embroiled in worry and stress over this case. Not only were we fighting about a tenancy agreement and the damage to our home, I never believed I would be in a position where I was actually suing Southampton Football Club.

My father-in-law, Bill, had been a season-ticket holder for years, since days long before Karen and I met. We were all Saints fans through and through. We always had a close relationship with the club during my time as a player, a coach, an ex-player and as supporters.

We had no ill feelings towards the club, only towards my tenant, but it did mean none of us could enjoy a very successful era on the pitch as Southampton rose back to the Premier League. This whole era is like a void in my mind. I couldn't watch the club I love. I was banned.

* * *

I always felt able to cope with football's various lows, whether they be injuries or red cards and suspensions, or even when I was dropped from the team. I was conditioned to respond to them in a positive way.

Losing the business was a very different scenario. It had an enormous impact on us all. My building company went into liquidation as an aftermath of the 2008 financial crisis, while we were in legal dispute with Nicola Cortese.

There were massive financial implications because we had personal guarantees with the bank and, ultimately, we had to sell the house. It wasn't a pleasant experience. It was the lowest point in our lives, full stop. I will always be grateful for our wonderful friends who stuck by us, and the inner circle of the family shone through. We pulled together and we made it through.

Ideas about what to do next had been bubbling away in the back of my mind for years. After my year at Eastleigh, I tried to keep fit with the odd charity game, going to the gym, doing things to keep in shape and live a healthy lifestyle.

Luke was growing up and I became drawn into coaching again. I went from standing on the touchline cheering him on, to taking a few training sessions in the evenings, to helping to run the team, Dougland.

I loved it. We had such a good bunch of lads, who were not only good players, but got on really well off the pitch. At times when I was coaching them in training or during a match, I would laugh to myself at some of the banter flying around. They went through the age groups together and moved to Romsey Town at Under-18s level to join a bigger set-up with a pathway to men's football, and I went with them because I wanted to see it through.

The coaching continued when Matt and I set up a football academy with two others. I was both a director and a head coach. I had come to accept there was life after football and, amazing as it seemed to me, there was a lot more out there to experience. But I still felt a lack of fulfilment from coaching and business interests. I started to look for a physical test. Going for a run or going to the gym did not give me the same focus or the sense of satisfaction I craved.

So I ran the London Marathon in 2006. Maybe that planted a seed. I enjoyed the training, working towards it, and was able to raise some money towards a local charity where I was a patron. Karen, Luke, Kenzie and myself all travelled into London and stayed in a hotel near Regents Park. On the day of the race, I jumped on the tube and made my way down to the start. I ran the course in three-and-a-half hours and absolutely loved the whole occasion.

* * *

The marathon has always been the ultimate test of endurance running and I was keen to do another one, perhaps in a different city. But at the same time, people were also running longer distances or combining disciplines and doing triathlons and some other more bizarre stuff. David Walliams, the television personality, had recently swum across the English Channel and the Strait of Gibraltar for Comic Relief charities.

I became intrigued and began to wonder about pushing at my own physical boundaries. How would I respond to a challenge like that? What were my limits? I wanted to do something to push me beyond anything I had experienced before.

It was brewing within me for years. I would mention it every so often to Karen and we talked about different things but they all seemed to be so huge. It was impossible to know where to begin, or how we would commit to such a mammoth task.

But Karen, Luke and Kenzie were all behind me and, over time, the thoughts and conversations became distilled into an idea to run across the country to all 20 Premier League grounds. It seemed to be a nice link to my past as a player.

I had absolutely no idea how far it was likely to be. The concept was in place before any distances were calculated. When we first mapped the route it was coming in at about 1,000 miles in total, at close to 50 miles a day if we were going to complete it in three weeks but were helped when Norwich were relegated at the end of the 2013–14 season. This came as a quite a relief. No offence to Canaries fans, I like them as a club despite my three red cards against them, but from the perspective of the challenge, it was just a long way from the other grounds. Running to Swansea in the west of Wales was challenging enough without having to run off to Norfolk. Cardiff and Fulham also went down to the Championship that year, while Leicester, Burnley and QPR went up. Overall, the promotion and relegation results definitely reduced my mileage. Norwich, however, would get its revenge on me in the second challenge.

The next thing was to tell friends what I proposed to do. That's when it felt like a definite commitment. I was accountable and did not want to break my word. The big push I needed came from Graham Lycett, who was the father of a boy I was coaching at our academy. Graham had a business in digital marketing, and he listened to the idea and his advice was to launch a website and generate some publicity because we were going to need sponsors.

This kick-started the operation. The search for a sponsor to cover the cost of vehicles, fuel and our accommodation as we moved around the country for three weeks led us to 4Com, a telecommunications company who were sponsoring our academy.

Not only did they agree to give us financial support but Daron Hutt, the managing director of the company, also introduced us to Dean Cartledge. 'You're going to need someone like Deano,' he said at our very first meeting, and gave us permission to bring him on board as our route manager, although he turned out to be a whole lot more than that.

Deano fine-tuned all the logistics of the challenge. He identified the route, the checkpoints and the places to start and finish each day. He even spent his weekends driving large sections of the route to ensure it was safe for me to run on. He is a Hull City supporter and, more importantly for the sake of the challenge, a former regimental sergeant major and army commando who had done a few fundraising challenges over the years.

He was a gem of a find. We set the start date for August, to coincide with the opening weekend of the 2014–15 Premier League season. Suddenly we were on the move and putting together a team.

It was all incredibly exciting and time to step up the training. I had been running on trails in the woods, often with Ben, our black Labrador, for company. He was fit and could run with me for four or five miles. It was perfect, although my approach was a bit naïve. I ran for 10 or 12 miles one day and then eased off the next day, until I sought some professional advice and was told to step it up. I needed to be doing some 20, 30 and 40-milers back-to-back to condition my body to the rigours of the challenge. That was useful to know and I ramped up the distances.

* * *

Not long after Nicola Cortese stepped down as chairman of Southampton, the club made contact and said they would like to welcome me back. They said they realised it might be difficult but there was an olive branch and I was glad to accept.

It was nice to end an unhappy time and go back to watching and cheering on the team again. They were back in the Premier League and performing well. As a family of Saints supporters, we had missed out on their successful climb back to the top flight.

Under Mauricio Pochettino, they finished eighth and then came in seventh and sixth in two years under Ronald Koeman. Sixth was their best finish since 1985, back when Lawrie McMenemy was still in charge and I was starting my apprenticeship on the YTS.

They returned to European football and to Wembley Stadium in the League Cup Final under Claude Puel. I was there on commentary duties for BT Sport as they played the final against Manchester United, a repeat of the 1976 FA Cup Final. Unfortunately, on this occasion, Southampton were beaten 3–2, a late winner headed in by Zlatan Ibrahimovic.

I was covering Saints quite often in my various media roles and Cortese's departure meant I could get involved again with the Saints Foundation, helping them to transform lives in the local community. This was something I was passionate about when I was club captain. I've since been made an official ambassador for the Foundation along with Kenzie, who also works closely with them.

Southampton became integral to my challenges. Mo Gimpel, who served for many years on the medical staff, helped me find a physio. Mo had been at the club in my playing days and promised to gauge interest among the part-time physios. He suggested having a chat with Kelly Rutledge, who was a young sports therapist working with one of the academy sides. It proved to be another wonderful find.

Kelly lived near Basingstoke and was interested in getting involved. She was the last of the on-road team to join the challenge we were calling 'Benali's Big Run'. We met her for the first time at St Mary's when we did a trial run, with support vehicles, through Hampshire covering the route we intended to follow on the last day of the event. She has a great personality and, of course, provided us with the medical skills we could not have done without. Kelly would become a loyal member in the team. Like others, she joined us on a voluntary basis and even took annual leave from her job to support us.

* * *

As club captain, I became heavily involved in Southampton's charity work during my career, regularly organising player visits to hospitals and hospices, which in turn brought me into contact with other charities. I became a patron of the Dave Wellman Cancer Trust and ran the London Marathon for them in 2006.

The challenge I was planning provided the perfect platform for me to raise funds and awareness for another good cause. We went into partnership with Cancer Research UK. Like most people, the disease touched us as a family – Karen had lost both her grandfathers to cancer.

It all began to come together. I met two women from the staff of Cancer Research UK in the Chilworth Manor hotel. I told them my plan and I told them I was looking to raise a million pounds, and they were enthusiastic about the project. One of them, Di Platt, went on to accompany us at various stages of the fundraising process. Di, along with other staff at the charity, gave us incredible support. They promised to get right behind us and were true to their word. We forged a great relationship.

Karen immersed herself in meetings and correspondence. All conversations in the house, whether we were eating breakfast or dinner, watching television or lying in bed, revolved around the same topic, every day for months.

The energy and unwavering support from Karen, Luke and Kenzie was so important. The kids gave up so much of their time to commit to this for months before, and I can honestly say we would never have got it off the ground without them.

After our initial calculations were helped by Norwich's relegation, Deano was able to finalise a route covering 838.15 miles, the equivalent of about 32 marathons, in three weeks. This worked out at an average of almost 40 miles a day.

The mileage alone was a daunting prospect and none of us could be sure what lay ahead. We were stepping into the unknown. How was my body going to react? What was I capable of doing? This was a leap of faith. Logistically, how would it all come together? We would learn many things. Only at the end would we realise how little we knew at the outset. We knew next to nothing.

8

THE BIG RUN

'One thing about working with a professional athlete on something like this is that they come into it with an assumed level of ability. They assume they can do it. The challenges taken on by Franny, however, were seriously extreme endurance challenges. While footballers can cover around 6 miles during a 90-minute game, chasing a ball around on a grass pitch is a very different discipline to running on the streets for 40 miles day after day after day.

The distances look enormous, because they are enormous, and training requires a different approach. It is easy to panic and fear you're not doing enough and then you end up doing too much. This was Franny all over. You won't complete the challenge if you don't reach the starting line. So it was important to create the right environment for him.

Once you've done that, the great thing about working with a professional athlete is that they understand what hard work is all about. They know nothing good comes easy. You don't have a successful career as a professional footballer if you don't work hard. That was the bonus with Franny.'

Professor Greg Whyte OBE,
physical activity expert and leading sports scientist

At 6 a.m. on Sunday 24 August, 2014, we gathered at the Sir Bobby Robson statue outside St James' Park in Newcastle and my old teammate and friend, Alan Shearer, officially launched the challenge.

Alan waved us on our way. It was an early start for him after appearing on *Match of the Day* the night before and I appreciated him making the effort to lend his support. Newcastle United were preparing to play their first game of the season against Manchester City, and would not allow us inside the ground, which didn't make for an auspicious opening to the event.

But we were up and running. Quite literally. These were the first steps on a long road and it was nice to have my family, my team and supporters from Cancer Research UK and a BBC television crew to wish me well. The plan was to reach Southampton, more than 800 miles and 21 days later, arriving at St Mary's Stadium during half time of a game coincidentally against Newcastle.

Obviously, I had attempted nothing like this before. I was 45 years old and more than eight years had passed since I ran the London Marathon. This was altogether different. I had been training, but the furthest I ever covered in training was 40 miles, which was in fact more like two 20-milers with a bit of lunch in between.

People had warned me about the enormity of the challenge I had taken on, including a sports scientist I knew through football and had bumped into on my way to addressing a group of local businessmen in a conference room at a hotel.

I was hoping to generate interest and, ideally, a little more sponsorship, and I saw this guy as I was walking into the venue. We shook hands and chatted briefly about my challenge. He said, 'Franny, please don't go in that room and tell them you're going to run 40 miles a day for three weeks.' He said it was impossible. He said I wouldn't complete it.

I had already been to see Professor Greg Whyte, the sports scientist involved in some of the Sport Relief and Comic Relief endurance challenges with celebrities such as Davina McCall and David Walliams. Luke and I visited his clinic in London and he put me through a series of tests to be sure my body was in good condition. I picked his brains and he gave me a useful insight into what to expect, how to prepare and how to train.

Professor Whyte did not tell me not to do it, but he also advised me to think carefully about the mileage. He definitely knew much more about this sort of thing than I did and his sage advice helped me understand just what I was undertaking.

I had no idea whether or not my body would stand up to it. There were no shortage of doubts in my mind even before this random encounter at the hotel, but it only served to reinforce the part of my brain that was always thinking, 'I'll show you.'

Through my entire football career, there were people who knocked me. People who doubted me. People who criticised me. They told me what I could not do and I always used that to motivate me. So, I walked into that conference room, addressed the audience and told them exactly what I intended to do.

There was no backing out now. The challenge was set. I had trained hard and wasn't about to back down. I was going to give it my best shot. I wasn't about to let any negative thoughts into my head. Easier said than done, of course, because having seriously cranked up the distances I was running in training, I felt a twinge in my right knee just five days before we were due to start. More than a twinge. In fact, quite a bad pain.

I went to see the medical team at Southampton FC and they sent me to see a consultant who took a scan and said there were a few issues in there. He recommended cortisone jabs, with which I was all too familiar from my playing career. I knew that was never a great thing to do because you mask the problem rather than heal it but we were low on options so I agreed.

On Thursday morning, it felt twice as bad. I could barely walk. On Friday, when the BBC, ITV and Sky were coming to film me running

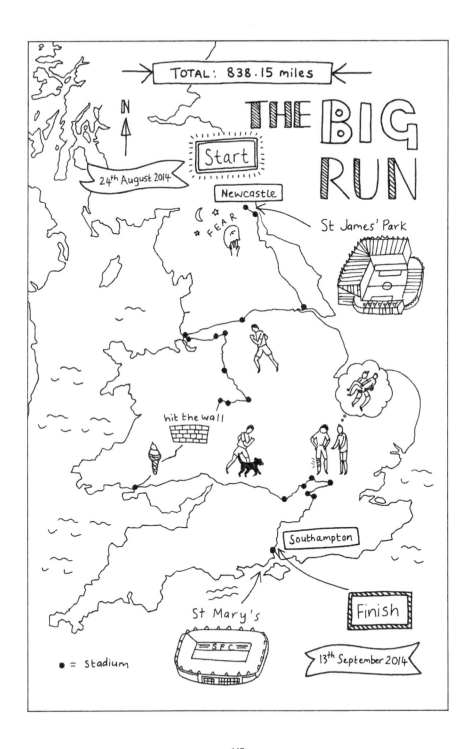

through Southampton Common, I was in quite a lot of discomfort and limping slightly as I jogged along. They must have thought I was having a laugh about running more than 800 miles.

The next day we travelled to Newcastle with my leg extended, hoping the injection would work and, when I went to bed, I still wasn't entirely sure if I was going to make it to the starting line.

I would have had no choice but to pull out if I was feeling the same way in the morning. I went to sleep and hoped for the best. When I woke up it felt like a brand new knee. It felt amazing. The cortisone must have kicked in. All the drama made us realise we had no contingency plan. We were learning on the job and increasingly aware of the size of the undertaking.

* * *

One thing none of us quite appreciated was the sheer length of the days. I ran for eight hours on Day One, 12 miles from Newcastle to the Stadium of Light in Sunderland, then south for another 28 miles to finish for the day in Albert Park, in Middlesbrough. This would become the norm. Stoppages to take on food and drink and to have treatment for blisters consumed time. Then, having reached our final destination for the day, we'd be phoning restaurants searching to find somewhere open for dinner. If I climbed into bed before 11 o'clock I was lucky.

Whenever we reached a football club, we would pause and pose for photographs and media opportunities and I started seizing up as my body cooled down. This was most severe in London where the clubs were closer together. We went to Arsenal, Tottenham, West Ham, Chelsea and Crystal Palace all in one day. By this stage, we were calling ahead to ask them to supply an exercise bike so I could keep my legs going. I would be pedalling away while talking to the local media. The publicity was important to raise as much money as possible.

A big part of my routine was the ice bath. We had an inflatable tub like a paddling pool, which the team would pump up and fill with water and ice each day, and position at the finishing point. As soon as my run was over, I would lower myself into the icy water, wincing at the pain and gasping for breath, and sit there shivering for five, six or seven minutes until Kelly was satisfied. I did not encounter ice baths during my playing career, at least, not until I went back to Southampton for preseason training when I was considering a comeback under Harry Redknapp. Even then, ice baths were a quick plunge in a wheelie bin full of cold water but here on the Big Run it was to be a vital part of my recovery process. The theory is that the very cold water will reduce any inflammation caused by micro muscle damage. It will also constrict the blood vessels and as they warm again, they gently open up, increasing the blood flow by way of a gentle surge of oxygen and nutrients through the system. Without it, there was no way I would have been able to run again the next day.

Another important piece of kit on all my challenges was my travel bed. It was a sleeping bag contraption – a mattress with a pillow and quilt attached, which we would set up on the floor of the hotel room. The idea came from Southampton FC who had picked it up from the cyclists at Team Sky. Quality rest was valuable, they said, and this was a good way to ensure you slept on the same surface every night. You knew exactly what you would be climbing into rather than taking your chances on different hotel beds. I slept on it for a few weeks before the challenge started and nicknamed it the 'marshmallow bed' as it was so incredibly soft and comfortable.

At the end of the first day, when I climbed into the marshmallow bed, inside a room at the Thistle Hotel in Middlesbrough, I was utterly exhausted and yet unable to switch off and sleep. I was tossing and turning. My mind was whirring. The thought of getting up in just a few hours' time and doing it all over again, and doing it every day for another 20 days, was simply too much. I simply could not get my head around it. I was in turmoil.

Karen was in the bed next to me. She asked me if I was OK. I tried to explain. I'm not sure I would have been making much sense but my wife got out of her bed and into the marshmallow bed with me. She gave me a cuddle, a few gentle words of encouragement. She said, 'You've done what you've done today, so you know you can do it. Don't look at it as a three-week challenge, just take it one day at a time. Rest tonight, get up tomorrow and do it again. I know you can do it.'

We all had doubts and fears but nobody was airing them. Karen has since told me she really didn't believe a word of what she was saying at the time. Quite the opposite, in fact, she was very concerned. She thought there was no way I could punish myself in this way for another 20 days.

Without her support and encouragement at that point, I'm not sure I could have gone a step further. Imagine that, after all the fuss and fanfare. After all those grand declarations about running to every Premier League ground and how we would raise a million pounds, it would have been over after one day. She has always been my tower of strength.

Karen soothed my mind and I drifted off, able to catch a few hours of rest. I would learn more about training my mind. From then on, I did not look forward more than one day at a time. I would break down the day and focus on getting through the next few hours or the next few miles. Sometimes, when I was struggling, or when my knee started to flare up again, I would focus on nothing more than putting one foot in front of the other.

* * *

It was unlike anything I'd been through in football. I was ready for physical pain but knew nothing about the mental grind. You glance at your watch and you've 'only' done 10 miles. There are up to another 30 to go. Your body aches, you are tired and your feet are blistering but you have to keep on running for six more hours.

At the very start of the process I set my mind on the target of a million pounds and I wasn't about to quit, but I realised just what a serious commitment this was going to be when I posed for a photograph near Burnley to show we had reached the £30,000 mark. Thoughts flashed back to the first meeting with Cancer Research UK. I told them I was aiming to raise a million. They nodded their approval and looked at each other as if to say, 'Does he know what he's talking about?' The truth was I didn't.

I was learning, though. Learning fast. Much of my time was spent running on country roads, often without pavements, and I found it is draining when you have to pay complete attention to every single vehicle, just in case the driver has failed to notice you and you have to take evasive action by leaping into the verge or hedgerow. There were some roads when the traffic was too lively and I had a few hairy moments. There was no shortage of abuse from drivers either, beeping their horns and showing me the full range of hand gestures.

A wrong turn on the A40 in London was completely my fault. I was running with Matt Le Tissier and a couple of Saints fans who had joined us, and we ended up going onto the inside lane of the dual carriageway and onto a busy flyover. That wasn't too clever and didn't go down well with the motorists. It seemed like an age before we reached the slip-road and were able to come off. I was expecting to see blue flashing lights and the police demanding to know what on earth we were doing.

Deano had taken great care to map the route, keeping me away from the steepest climbs and, where possible, away from heavy traffic and sometimes onto a canal towpath to ease the stress. I would be able to switch off and enjoy the tranquillity.

There were times when I wanted to run on my own. From a safety point of view, I opted to run without any music. I was on public roads and didn't want earphones in. In the North Yorkshire Moors and the Brecon Beacons, I discovered beautiful parts of the country. I would try to lose myself in the scenery and the surroundings.

My son Luke and daughter Kenzie ran with me. Luke was crashing out 20 miles a day on a regular basis with hardly any training. Karen, who loathes running, was out running five miles a day. On one occasion, she ran for 11 miles. Then she never ran again until the next challenge.

My support team were working around the clock and surviving on less than five hours' sleep a night. They would go to bed after midnight and be up at 4.30 a.m. Karen would often end the day sitting in the bath in the hotel room, washing our kit by hand and trying to have it dry before we left at 6 a.m. the next day.

We were operating with only three or four sets of kit. Sometimes the support team would drive by with a pair of my shorts fluttering from the wing mirrors of the car as they tried to dry them.

Every morning and every night, Kelly gave me treatment. On top of this, she took care of my nutritional needs. She kept a diary of everything I ate. She had to make sure her medical bag was in check and ready for the following day. Most nights, her dinner would sit on the side, still untouched at midnight because there was no time to eat it.

Luke and Kenzie were filming the whole thing, and were always dashing off to find electricity to charge our various devices, blogging or vlogging, and searching for WiFi capable of downloading the files and sending them off to the media outlets we had promised to keep updated.

At one hotel where the WiFi wasn't the best, Luke's computer told him it was going to take three years to transmit a video file he was trying to send. One of our gadgets was a tracking device enabling people to follow my progress online. It was 'Where's Franny?' rather than 'Where's Wally?' and it seemed to be working because gradually more people started to come out and show support.

I was running into Birmingham along one of the canals when I noticed someone in the distance wearing a Saints shirt. As I got closer, he shouted, 'Hey, Franny, it works.' He'd been following me online and worked out I'd be coming this way. He ran with me for a while and his local knowledge helped me find my way to Villa Park.

* * *

As I covered the miles on the streets and footpaths, the team were getting into scrapes of their own. Looking after me in unfamiliar parts of the country while suffering from sleep deprivation was proving to be a stressful experience. One day, Karen and Kelly were so hopelessly lost they were in a different country, having taken a wrong turn and driven across the border. I was in Wales and they were back in England.

Hire cars were collateral damage. We had to abandon one with its clutch burned out, on a steep zig-zag climb out of Hebden Bridge on Day Five. They had been crawling along behind me as I struggled on an uphill stretch between Hull to Burnley. The car simply chugged to a halt and we had to leave it.

When Karen drove the wrong way down a one-way street and found other motorists beeping and waving she smiled and waved back. She thought they were honking their support rather than trying to stop her.

Luke misplaced a £5,000 camera, kindly lent to us by Veho, Southampton's shirt sponsors at the time. We were in London and, to make matters worse, it was the first day the people from Veho were due to join us.

We were at West Ham before anyone noticed it was missing. Luke figured it must've been pushed under the bed in a cluttered hotel room amid the confusion of another night on the road. He tried to call the hotel, but no one answered. He set off back across the capital towards Marylebone in heavy traffic, panic rising. It took him a long time to get there but the camera was exactly where he thought, under a bed and was safely retrieved.

I didn't hear about any of this until we were on a holiday weeks later. So much was happening and there wasn't time to tell me everything.

There were also times, I discovered, when they deliberately kept things from me, and times when I became the butt of their jokes. I've never been much of a diva but the kids teased me because I started to refuse the Haribo sweets they were handing me from the car window and threw them back, saying, 'You know I don't like the green ones.'

Once, I threw a bit of a hissy fit when they passed me Luke's sunglasses instead of mine, which seemed to cause a great deal of amusement. The two pairs of glasses were almost identical. Luke's had a tortoiseshell frame and mine were black. That was the only difference. I don't know why but the black ones had become part of my routine and, in my tired mental condition, it was vitally important for me to have them. 'The black ones,' I snapped. 'I need the black ones.'

* * *

The strain was starting to show and I reached breaking point at the end of Day 12, a full day on the road with no football grounds to break the monotony as we covered the long haul of 115 miles between The Hawthorns at West Bromwich Albion and Swansea's Liberty Stadium.

The finishing point on that day was in the car park of a pub called the Boat Inn at Whitney-on-Wye, in Herefordshire. There were beautiful views of the river and a small campsite where I could have my ice bath, shower, change into fresh clothes, and eat something before we rested for the night at our accommodation nearby.

This was another chore for the support team. Each day they had the ice bath pumped up and ready for me to sink into but our route wasn't always planned according to the proximity of ice and water. The finishing point might be a car park, a village green, a football club or a lay-by, and very rarely was it the hotel where we would spend the night. Wherever it might be, they had to ferry the gallons of water and buckets of ice to the inflatable bath. On the rare occasion we did finish at a hotel, it was a real bonus as I had the luxury of getting out of an ice bath and straight into a hot shower. It also meant the team were back in the hotel a little earlier and not stood on the side of the road waiting for me.

That day, Karen knew I was starting to really struggle and had gone ahead with Kenzie to the finish line. They had tried to lift my spirits by persuading the drinkers and staff in the Boat Inn to come outside and cheer me home. I don't know what they were expecting but I'm sure they had not bargained on the physical and emotional wreck that came staggering into view. I collapsed to my knees and into the arms of my wife. I plunged into the ice bath, completely out of it.

Kenzie came across to record an interview. It was something we did at the end of each day. All she said was, 'Hey Dad, how was today?' That was it, I went to pieces. Out of nowhere, the pain and the psychological struggle of the day came washing over me and I started to sob uncontrollably.

I've never been a crier, so for my family and the support team to suddenly see me like this hit them hard. Kenzie started to cry as well, and gave me a hug. The video is tough to watch back, seeing us both crying while she is hugging me over the ice bath and it resonated when it went out on our social media and across news outlets. I think for the first time the pain I was in was becoming apparent to everyone at home.

The drinkers from the pub were still looking on, sipping at their pints. Karen told them I usually came bounding in, all smiles and offering handshakes of gratitude for their support and here I was, broken. Physically and emotionally, this was my lowest point. The day had been long and exhausting, another hard day of 40 miles, with much of the route out of Kidderminster uphill towards the Welsh border.

Time had dragged by slowly and everything seemed to be a huge effort. I was just over halfway through the entire challenge and there was still a long way to go. I was far from Swansea and then there would be another long slog to cover 185 miles across the country to London before I turned home towards Southampton.

There were times when I would be running along and, suddenly, I would burst into tears and I wasn't always sure why. Thoughts poured into my head: What was I doing? Why was I doing it? Karen's grandfathers had passed away from cancer, we had lost close friends to the illness, and we'd met cancer patients every day along the way, listening to their stories. The emotion was overwhelming at times.

Guilt welled up: Why was I putting my team through this? It can't have been easy for them to see me like this. Doubt lingered: Could I keep going? What if I failed? Would the charity still get the money? Could I still help the people I'd met that morning?

I used that to push me on. On the better days, I flipped that easily into motivation. Don't stop. Don't give up because if you give up the donations won't come in. We soon discovered there was a clear correlation between the distress I was in and the donations we were receiving. The worse my condition the more money came in. I had to keep going.

I passed out under the shower on the camp site next to the Boat Inn. I could feel it coming over me and I sat down to avoid falling. Karen had gone off to get me some dry clothes and when she came back I was slumped against the wall in the shower.

We went into the pub for dinner. They had been so kind and welcoming, but I didn't even pick up my fork. I was finding it difficult to eat at this stage. I was running on empty. I could not stomach breakfast the next day either. Kelly and the team were becoming increasingly concerned that I was not taking in enough calories to provide the energy required to run the miles and keep up with the relentless schedule.

I started the next day running with Luke. He always brought me calmness with words of encouragement and inspiration. He's always been good with numbers and when I was thinking, 'Oh no, another 300 miles to go' he would be reeling off the distances already covered, totalling nearly 500 miles by this stage, and the pace we were setting and where we would be up to by the end of the day. He would say, 'You've done all that, Dad, you can make it to the end'. It reinforced the bond we have. He was worried and I knew we would both feel better by being together. At times, we chatted about anything just to take our minds off the endless miles. Other times we would run in silence.

I might catch myself shuffling along, eyes firmly fixed on the tarmac or pavement below me so I consciously tried to lift my head up and look around. We ran through some beautiful parts of the country and this stage through the Brecon Beacons was among the most stunning, in contrast to the morale inside the group, which was at its lowest ebb.

Karen and Kenzie were driving ahead to the first stopping point. We had been scheduled to meet up at a petrol station when Karen spotted the Llanfaes Dairy Shop, a lovely ice-cream parlour in the town of Brecon. They called Deano and Kelly who were in another car, staying close to me and decided to stop there instead in the hope I might be tempted to eat something, anything. It was a few yards before the petrol station and we were at a point where the most important thing was getting some fuel into my body.

Normally, I find it impossible to refuse ice cream and, once again, it seemed to do the trick. One scoop of vanilla and my appetite was back. We all had a chat and spirits were boosted. This was a big turning point. From here, I started to eat again, not huge amounts but at least I was taking on some much needed fuel and the team had a secret weapon now, ice cream.

It was a couple of days later, as we were making our run out of Wales, we were running along a narrow stretch of country road. On this lonely route, with nothing but rolling fields as far as you could see, there came into view an ice-cream van, parked in a lay-by ahead, shimmering like an oasis in the desert.

Deano had conjured it up apparently, but at the time I thought it a wonderful coincidence and that was a real tonic for me. I was so happy. Ice creams all round and I was on my way again. I began to wonder whether I should have organised to have an ice-cream van as one of the permanent support vehicles.

Di Platt and Shelley Thompson, from Cancer Research UK, were in constant communication with the team and they knew I was struggling. On Day 12, unbeknown to me, they made their way to Wales and joined us as permanent support for the third and final week. These displays of solidarity really helped to boost spirits in the camp and kept me going. I hope everyone knows how much it meant to me.

My in-laws, Bill and Eileen, arrived with our family friends, Wayne and Michelle Hausen, and they brought Ben, our beloved black Labrador with them. It was a wonderful surprise. Ben suddenly appeared as I ran out of a little village in Wales. He even had his own specially adapted team T-shirt to wear.

We all had dinner together at the team hotel and the next day I ran through the Cotswolds with Ben at my side, my trusty companion who had accompanied me on so many training runs in the woods near home.

Bill caught the bug and decided he would stay with us when the others went home but he had only brought clothes for a one-night stay. The Hawaiian shorts he wore for the rest of the week became a great source of amusement.

Word was spreading about the challenge and new faces were appearing every day. Matt Le Tissier completed two 20-mile sections and that was quite a commitment. Some might say it was more than he ever ran as a player. I couldn't ever describe him as a good runner but he was more comfortable with this 6 mph pace than the pace we used to run when we trained at Southampton. His wife, Angie, also regularly met up with us and ran with me.

Matt was with me on a day when I was feeling particularly rough and the knee flared up out of nowhere and stopped me in my tracks. We had gone off course once, adding unnecessary miles to the total and making us late for a roadside TV interview with Sky Sports. Deano drove to rescue us. We crammed into the back of his car with a bicycle and bags of kit and he dropped us back on the route. We were making our way into London, following a canal path under the M25 when I suddenly pulled up in pain.

Matt was hopping around, unsure whether to run ahead or call the team. He knew I'd been having trouble with my knee. I just needed a minute to compose myself before I could get moving again, and he came over to me and said, 'Mate, you know I'll carry you if you want me to.'

The sentiment was greatly appreciated. I could tell he meant it. I told him if I'd known he was willing to carry me I would have pulled up a few miles sooner! Fortunately, it didn't come to that. The pain eased and we got a message through to Kelly who was waiting with Deano at the other end of the canal path. She ran in our direction to find us, gave me some treatment and we were moving again.

The knee stopped me a few times. We would have to take a break so Kelly could treat me with a portable ice pack, which was usually enough to settle it down. I popped some painkilling tablets but it was mostly a question of running through the pain. I was always conscious of the time pressure. I tried to kick on with the pace in those periods where I was feeling really good, in the hope it might give us some more down time and rest at the end of the day.

* * *

Crystal Palace was our last stop in London and, as we turned towards Southampton, this was the point when I knew nothing was going to stop me. I ran the last three days thinking I had cracked it. The bulk of the miles were behind me. I was 18 days into the run and I knew I could do it. This swell of confidence felt amazing.

I never took anything for granted. I knew the knee could flare up out of nowhere. But these were moments to savour. They were miniscule in the bigger picture of turmoil and grind and the battles with your mind and body, but they were golden moments. They felt great. Pain-free in a fluent rhythm. I probably wasn't flying but it felt good. It was a great place to be.

I wasn't as concerned as Kelly was about a redness developing on one of my shins. To be honest it just blurred in with all the other aches and pains around my body but she was worried I might have an infection and we kept a close eye on it. I took some painkillers and Kelly wrapped it tightly in a bandage to keep the swelling down.

We found out afterwards that it was a stress fracture but nothing was going to stop us at this stage. We had broken the back of the challenge and there was plenty of support as we weaved out way through the villages of Hampshire.

Lots of people with Southampton connections had been out to support me during the challenge. Charlie Austin came to see me at QPR, and Danny Ings at Burnley, who were the only club to make a monetary contribution to the cause on this challenge. James Beattie was manager of Accrington Stanley at the time and he came out and ran with me into Burnley. Another former Saints player, Dean Hammond, ran almost a half marathon with me into Leicester where he was playing.

There were other familiar football faces. Gary Mabbutt gave us a wonderful warm welcome at Tottenham, and we saw Jason Cundy at Chelsea. I often chat with him on his radio show on talkSPORT. There was a lot of support from the football community. It always gave me a lift to see a fresh face and have a different conversation and then we'd be on our way again.

Ralph Krueger, the then Saints chairman, was among those who came out to run with me on the final leg, into Southampton.

The rush of adrenalin, knowing I was going to make it to the finish line, was overriding any feelings of pain or discomfort from the stress fracture. Had there been another week to go it might have been very different.

The run into Southampton was amazing. I ran the final 33-mile section from Bentley in Surrey, which was shorter than the distances covered on any of the previous days because we were finishing early to coincide with kick-off.

Running through the streets to the stadium, I was amazed by the sheer volume of people lining every street and gathering outside every pub to cheer us on. There was a party atmosphere with cars honking their horns and people joining in to run with us, whether it was for a few miles or a few hundred yards. I felt like a politician, everyone was trying to shake my hand and congratulate me. We reached St Mary's Stadium a few minutes before kick-off to find thousands waiting outside to welcome us home.

With the help of Saints, we were able to bring the challenge to an official close with a lap of the pitch at half time. My spine tingled as I ran to the finish line. Even the Newcastle fans gave me a round of applause, which was kind of them considering they were 2–0 down and a long way from home. The challenge had started at St James' Park on the opening day of the season, so there was a nice symmetry to the fact they were the visitors as I came in to finish.

Southampton made announcements urging fans to stay in their seats to see me arrive at half time, which I later found out cost them tens of thousands in lost food and drink revenue. It was a nice gesture and summed up what a truly special club it is.

There was a pitch-side interview and then into the ice bath for the last time. I had done it. Slowly, the reality dawned on me. I showered and hobbled around some of the hospitality suites in my tracksuit and flip-flops to talk to some of the supporters. The euphoria washed over me. And the relief. The challenge was complete. After three weeks on the road, it was good to walk in through the front door after all those hotel rooms. It was time to rest. Time for some home comforts.

9

THE BIG RACE

'Dad encountered some really dark moments during his first challenge. Every ounce of his energy was gone, he was exhausted and at times he could hardly even articulate a response. One day in particular, we thought he'd met his threshold when he collapsed into Mum's arms and began to sob. I couldn't recall ever seeing Dad cry and here he was on his hands and knees sobbing his heart out. It was incredibly tough to witness.

We were so proud of everything he was doing but at what point do you stop encouraging him to persevere through the pain and say, "Enough is enough, let's call it a day." Even if we had told him to pack it in, we all knew, deep down, that wasn't going to happen.

When he told us he wanted to take on another challenge, none of us were remotely surprised. He's never been one to sit around and do nothing and as much as he loves to test himself physically, his main drive has always been to help better the lives of other people.

You could search this whole world over and you would still struggle to find another Francis Benali.'

Kenzie Benali, Franny's daughter

I woke up in my own bedroom for the first time in three weeks but not quite in the luxury of my own bed. For recovery reasons, I was still on the marshmallow bed but it was a wonderful feeling to roll over and have a lie-in.

There was a glow of satisfaction and achievement. We had made it. I was happy not to have to get up and run, but from the moment I opened my eyes I knew I wanted to do it again. I wanted to take on another challenge.

I was picking up vibes from my football days. It was the buzz from being part of a team. The bond of a group of people together on the road, living in each other's pockets, going out on a limb for one another. This time, side by side with my family.

I was missing it already. I missed the excitement of another day on the challenge. I missed the camaraderie of the life on the road. We had shared an experience none of us will ever forget, for good or bad. For months, we were planning, all working towards the same thing. Then there was the period of intensity when we were in the heart of the challenge and every waking thought was dedicated to its completion.

Then, it was over. I reached the finish line, shook hands and we all went our different ways. Then, nothing. Only a hollow feeling. I soon found out I wasn't the only one going through these emotions. Everyone else in the team was missing it, too. By the end of the third challenge, there was a name for it. We started to call it the Iron Fran Blues.

* * *

Our first challenge was barely over and I was already making up my mind to definitely do another.

The other factor driving me on was the fundraising. We were nowhere near the target. After the Big Run Gala Dinner at St Mary's Stadium to celebrate the challenge, we were up to £265,000 – but I wanted to raise a million.

People were so extremely generous. We had raised a huge chunk of money but we were still a long way from the promise I made, and our ties to the Cancer Research UK charity were closer than ever. My father-in-law, Bill, was diagnosed with prostate cancer after the first challenge and two of our close friends also discovered they had cancer.

One of them, Vicky Chappell, was eight months younger than me. We first met her and her husband Stuart when he was general manager at the Grand Harbour Hotel in Southampton, we became great friends and remained in close contact when they moved away to London, and then Malta.

The other was Dave Hill, who was known to everyone as Big Dave, an ex-bouncer who drove for Alan Ball and then Matt Le Tissier. Dave looked as though he had stepped out of the cast of a Guy Ritchie gangster movie, with his imposing frame and a ring on every finger, but he was the exact opposite, a gentle giant who would do anything for anyone. He had driven Matt and Angie up to various locations to run with me on the first challenge. Dave died in May 2016, a few months before the second challenge, and was a great loss to all of us.

Everyone has these stories and we are no different to others. No family is untouched by the indiscriminate nature of cancer but there was no way I wanted to stop. I was more determined than ever to go again.

First, though, I needed to give my body and mind time to recover. I also had to give time to my family and to focus on gainful employment, which was coaching and some media work. While I was doing that, I considered what to do next. The question was constantly on my mind and I would bump into people and they would say, 'What you did was fantastic, what's next?'

Benali's Big Run went down well. I received a Cancer Research UK Flame of Hope for the fundraising effort and was the first recipient of the Barclays Spirit of the Game award from the sponsors of the Premier League at the time.

Somehow, I even beat Superman actor Henry Cavill to win the Celebrity Just Giving Fundraiser of the Year, and I thought it was going to have to be something equally extreme if we were to stay ahead of

Superman, and engage people and ask them to donate generously again. I had to make it bigger and crazier than the first one. I wanted to raise the bar but we had already set it quite high, certainly from an endurance perspective.

Karen joked that if only I had done a 10km (6-mile) Fun Run then at least we could have raised it to a marathon. She knew I wanted to do something else and she dreaded hearing what mad scheme I might come up with next. We went to see the movie 'Everest', and she was expecting me to come out of the cinema with a grand plan to set off on an expedition to the Himalayas in flip-flops or something equally implausible.

I did consider climbing a mountain. In my spare time, I researched various different events around the world, and thought of breaking the football link and doing something different.

The comedian Eddie Izzard set out in February 2016 to complete 27 marathons in 27 days in South Africa in tribute to Nelson Mandela, who spent 27 years of his life in prison in the fight against apartheid. What a phenomenal feat of endurance.

For a long period, I was seriously considering an event called the Badwater Ultramarathon, a 135-mile race through California's Death Valley, which takes place every July when temperatures can reach 54ºC (130ºF).

It is one of the most gruelling races anywhere, even for the top endurance runners, and this really caught my imagination until I discovered there was a stringent qualifying process and I couldn't be sure whether or not they would accept me on the basis of the Big Run.

Ultimately, I went around in a full circle and came back to the football theme. One thing I was sure about, I wanted to make it a shorter challenge than the first, mindful of the pressure on everybody's time.

I made a few calls to get the team back together again. Jo Dalton, who helped us with media in the first challenge, agreed to be our project manager and set up a brilliant three-man media team, Innes Marlow, Paul Watts and Gregor Hannah, who all went above and beyond expectations.

Pete Dixon, who owns a digital advertising company called Maxx Media, donated so much time and money to the cause. Pete, who lost both his parents to cancer, arranged advertising to promote the challenge and boost donations. I spoke to a friend of mine, Paul Bradford, who owns Southern Communications Ltd and who agreed to be our main sponsor.

We cut this challenge down to a fortnight, but increased the mileage to about 1,400 miles to visit not only the 20 Premier League clubs, as before, but also the 24 clubs in the Championship. We also added the bike as an extra discipline.

We called it 'Benali's Big Race'. Over two weeks in October 2016, I ran a marathon every morning and then cycled a minimum of 75 miles each day.

* * *

To say I was a novice when it came to cycling is a bit of an understatement. I was the proud owner of a Raleigh Grifter as a boy, but didn't own a road bike until I agreed to join the Saints Foundation for part of a ride from Southampton to Leicester in 2015. Someone at the club managed to source me a decent bike. It not only got me to Leicester but would ultimately get me through my next two ultra-endurance challenges.

There were new skills to learn and I had some embarrassing tumbles as I set off into the streets of Southampton in the early days of practice. It took time before I was accustomed to unclipping my feet from the pedals whenever I stopped at traffic lights. I would just topple sideways into the pavement or the road.

A good friend, Andrew Hartley, is a serious amateur cyclist. He is a very powerful rider who has taken part in countless races around the country and in Europe. He helped me to put a training schedule together and promised to come out to join me for a couple of days in the saddle once the challenge was under way.

His experience on the bike was invaluable. I was so hopelessly naïve. When he came to ride with me on Day Three, I had just completed 26.2

miles on foot. He found me scoffing food and taking a drink as I hurriedly changed out of my running kit and into my cycling gear in the back of one of the support cars.

It wasn't very glamorous. I had a 15-minute window between the two disciplines, and Karen would sit in the front and hold a towel across, trying to give me some privacy. Andrew had talked me through the importance of chamois cream, an ointment spread on the inside of cycling shorts and designed to eliminate chafing and saddle soreness. I had been applying this stuff liberally and still had the tub in my hand when he appeared that day. I showed it to him and asked, 'Is this what you use?'

He squinted at it. 'Yeah, I do use that.' He was half-laughing and half-wincing. 'I put it on my chain.' It was chain grease. I had been rubbing it into my nether regions for weeks in training. It had arrived amid the many boxes of supplies and donations we were grateful to receive. On reflection, I did think it was very sticky. The whole team were in hysterics and Karen joked, 'Well, at least we know nothing's going to rust down there.'

Thanks to Andrew, I discovered other useful tips and techniques. I learned all about the importance of closely following his back wheel to ride in his slipstream and conserve energy, and there were times when he instructed me to change my position. We might be riding through the open countryside on a breezy day, with a cross-wind, and he knew I was working harder than I had to so he would tell me to move alongside his back wheel, to shelter. Often we were travelling at 30 or 40 mph and there were times when I came perilously close to clipping his wheel just through fatigue or a lapse in concentration. That would have sent us both sprawling on the tarmac.

It was a steep learning curve and I was pleased when Andrew came out at the end of the challenge and said he thought my riding skills had improved tremendously. Maybe he was just being nice, but a big part of it was confidence and he helped me to build that. I trusted him and put my faith in him. You have to when you are a couple of inches from someone's back wheel, travelling at nearly 40 mph. If there is a pot hole, I can't see it. It is about trusting what he can see. He eased the mental strain by taking the decision-making away from me.

* * *

There was no Deano with us on this challenge, which was a big blow. Not only was he a key member of the team from the first challenge, brilliantly guiding us around the country, but he was a big character, kicking us up the backside in the nicest possible way when we needed to get moving or lifting the mood when we were low.

There were times when he had us rolling around in fits of laughter, especially when he performed his pretend daily vlogs at dinner, where he recapped the day's events in the style of an episode of 'Big Brother'.

Luke didn't find him quite so funny at 4.30 every morning when he woke him up with his alarm, which was a recording of the warning siren of an incoming missile attack from his army days.

It put everyone on a downer, particularly me, when he was not able to be part of the Big Race. It took me a while to get my head around the disappointment. I did see him at one point, though. He made his way up to the Midlands on a day off work, dressed-up as a workman, in a hi-vis vest, glasses and a flat-cap, and leapt out in the middle of a road waving a spirit level.

Deano's little appearance that day gave us a huge lift but we had to make do without his logistical skills. In his absence, we tried to make good use of technology. This challenge was going to be different because of the bike. I would be covering the miles much more quickly and that was going to make it more difficult for the support team to keep up.

We consulted Ordnance Survey and they offered to map out a route and programme it into the navigation device we had for the bike. This, in theory, would enable me to go off merrily into the distance following the sat nav instructions.

Unfortunately, that idea went out of the window almost immediately. I was only a few miles into the first ride and it was clearly not going to work. The route on the tracker did not resemble the actual road. I would come to a roundabout, for example, and be wondering which exit to take but on the device there was no roundabout. It was a technical issue but I didn't have time to stop and address it.

Cycling along, the device would flash with messages saying 'off route' but didn't reroute me. It just kept flashing away. Very quickly, it became impossible to use it.

This early technological setback to the logistical operation added pressure to the support team because, from this point, I would have to be following someone. Sometimes that was one of the support team in a car but there was also a lovely guy called Ian Smith who had emailed us offering to assist, and would prove to be a godsend.

Ian is a Saints fan, a retired police officer and a keen motorcyclist. He was in his late 60s at the time and I had been coaching his grandson Ewan at our football academy. He knew about our fundraising for Cancer Research UK because he followed the first challenge and came out to cheer us on at Durley near the end of the Big Run.

Ian's eldest son Paul twice recovered from Hodgkin's Lymphoma while in his 20s, and his daughter Lisa had been recently diagnosed with a brain tumour, on her 40th birthday. Cancer had touched his family and he wanted to support us.

We thought we had everything covered but we invited him along anyway. He came on his motorbike and, when the navigation technology failed, he essentially became my support rider for large parts of the journey. There were times when there were only the two of us out on the road. I could sight him and he was able to liaise with the rest of the team more easily than I could. He worked closely with Rob Pike, who had taken over in Deano's role as the route manager.

Rob, also ex-military and good to work with, came on board shortly before the challenge. He only had a limited time to work on the route. Each challenge definitely needed strong characters and organisation from the top down.

* * *

I was due to run a marathon every morning and cycle in the afternoons. By adding the Championship to the Premier League clubs, it meant there were 44 grounds to reach. To get us going, we started at the Vitality Stadium in Bournemouth on 2 October, 2016, and headed north towards Bristol City. Then it was over into Wales, to Cardiff and Swansea, and then back into England and around the country in a clockwise direction.

The route would take us over to Birmingham City, Aston Villa, West Brom and Wolves in the West Midlands, then north to Stoke, Manchester City, Manchester United, Liverpool, Everton and Wigan. Then onto Preston, Blackburn and Burnley, and over the Pennines to Newcastle before turning south to call at Sunderland, Middlesbrough, Hull, Leeds, Huddersfield, Barnsley, Rotherham and Sheffield Wednesday.

From Yorkshire we were bound for the East Midlands, to Nottingham Forest, Derby, Burton, and Leicester, then east to Norwich and Ipswich, and then back towards London for Tottenham, West Ham, Arsenal, Chelsea, Fulham, QPR, Brentford, Watford, Reading and Crystal Palace. The final stages would include Brighton and back to Southampton, again to tie in with a game on 16 October.

Another major problem with the route formulated by our navigation device was the gradient. The hills really hit us on that first day as we climbed towards Bristol. Some of them were brutal. In my wisdom, I had done the bulk of my training in the New Forest. The scenery is beautiful and the forest is quiet but it didn't take me long to realise my mistake. Compared to the rest of the country, it is as flat as a pancake so it was a hell of a shock when we encountered some serious hills. I really wasn't prepared for them.

Riding with Andrew on the first day, trying to follow roughly the same route thrown at us by the tracking device, he was convinced there must have been a better, flatter and more bike-friendly route so, when he went home, he started to study the plans and the maps and liaised closely with Rob on the route.

This is where Andrew became engrossed in the challenge. The bug had bitten, and he spent more time with us than he planned. He runs his own recruitment business so he was able to juggle commitments and would drive home after one ride, spend a day or two at work and then drive back to meet us again.

* * *

Injuries plagued this challenge and they kicked in immediately. There was a hamstring issue on my left leg from the second day and, before long, a problem with my Achilles tendon on the right leg.

In some ways, I found it more difficult approaching the second challenge. There was a novelty value to the first one. This time we knew more about what we were taking on but having encountered the problems I did on the first challenge, the closer we got to the second one I remembered the low points, and knew those really dark moments would be waiting for me again.

I knew there were going to be times when I would struggle physically or mentally, or both. Knowing what lay ahead made it harder and not easier. But I had gone into the challenge in good physical condition. Unlike the first challenge, there were no niggling issues. I had learned a lesson and tried to reach the start line in good shape.

I certainly did not anticipate an injury so early into the challenge. During the marathon on Day Two, I found myself unceremoniously face down on a picnic bench in Wales with Kelly trying to apply tape to the back of my leg to relieve the tension on my hamstring.

With my hairy legs, the tape refused to cling on and she was asking people to find her a razor blade so she could shave them. Matt Le Tissier was there to run with me and had hitched a lift with Gordon Watson, a.k.a. Flash, one of our old teammates from Saints.

Flash came to the rescue because there was a razor in his overnight bag. I'm not sure what was worse, borrowing it from him to shave my legs or handing it back to him afterwards for him to use later.

The hamstring was sore and it nagged away. I was confident it wasn't going to snap but it certainly made movement uncomfortable. Kelly was able to keep on top of it. Once the Achilles problem flared up, however, I was in much more pain and it was with me for every step of every marathon and every turn of the pedals on the bike rides. There was no respite.

Kelly strapped my ankle and cut a hole in the back of my running shoe to relieve pressure, but gradually it got worse until we reached Norwich. It had been a long and sapping ride in the wind into East Anglia. We were not far from the finish but my Achilles was badly swollen and bruised.

I woke in the night, about 3 a.m., in my marshmallow bed on the floor of the hotel room. I needed the toilet. I rolled from my mattress and onto the floor, stood up and collapsed immediately. My ankle simply gave way. I was in agony. It was so painful that I could not stand up.

I crawled to the toilet on all fours, crawled back to my bed and lay awake thinking. I could easily have given up. The temptation was so strong. My alarm would go off again in two hours and it would be time to get up and run another marathon. Outside the rain was torrential. I could hear it hammering down on the roof. I wasn't sure I could face another day on the road. Spirits were that low.

Besides the injury, we had been without Luke and Kenzie for a few days, and that felt like a blow to me. They left the challenge for a few days to complete a charity sky dive. It had been in their diaries for months and there was no way around it. We also lost Ian for a couple of days when his Honda Deauville broke down in the middle of the A1 during a rainstorm, only a few miles north of the Travelodge where we were to finish for the night.

The mechanical damage was the result of a heavy workload at slow speeds, for 10 to 12 hours at a time, and he had to push the bike across two lanes of thundering traffic and take refuge in a hedgerow for three hours as Rob made the calls to organise his roadside recovery. At least a passing motorist was kind enough to stop and offer him a hot cup of coffee.

Ian thought he had let the team down. Nothing could have been further from the truth. We would have been lost on many occasions without him. Like everyone else, he was gripped by the emotion of the team challenge.

The breakdown service took him back to Southampton and the Honda garage at Lowford were kind enough to fix the problem quickly and free of charge. He was back on the road within a few days, by the time we left Fulham.

* * *

Back in Norwich, I drifted back to sleep. When the alarm sounded and Kelly came in to start the daily treatment and preparation, my ankle was red and badly swollen. The injury was clear for her to see. I knew she was concerned. She had already conferred with the medical department at Saints. She strapped it up again in silence. It was all part of the routine.

I barely spoke. I wasn't in the mood for conversation and I was trying to stop negative thoughts from taking over my mind. I didn't want to give them a voice. I popped a couple of painkillers and set out on the run. There were only a few days to go before I could rest and recover, and I really did not want to quit.

There were always many obstacles across the challenges, points in the process where I could not be certain which way it was going to go.

This was one of those pivotal moments. All I could do was block out the pain.

We had no room for manoeuvre. No time to play with. There were two options: quit and concede defeat or keep going and stick to the schedule.

I had no idea if I was doing permanent damage by carrying on. If my Achilles was going to rupture, it would be the end of the challenge, there was no debate about that, but quitting has never been in my nature and I was determined to fight against it.

To block out the reality of the situation, I shut down my mind. It was something I learned to do over the course of the challenges. Almost as though I could switch off the pain. When I was really struggling, I would tend to go quiet and retreat into my own shell. I think it was all part of my 'shutting down' process.

I sometimes put on music as a distraction. I chose not to do this on the first challenge for safety reasons but I came to realise there were stretches where it was safe to have my earphones in. There were times when it was uplifting and helped me to establish my rhythm. I tried to listen to songs with a good tempo for my running, like Calvin Harris and Craig David, or a bit of old school RnB to lift my mood. I came to rely quite heavily on it.

One day, I turned my iPod on and found the battery was flat. I had forgotten to charge it properly overnight. Such a tiny setback could have a big impact on my frame of mind. It took me half an hour to sort my head out again.

More positively, I did not have the same problems getting fuel on board during this challenge. I was eating and drinking enough to keep me going, and I was back on the ice cream again. I've not been off it since, to be honest.

I knew our route and would visualise the badges of the clubs and tick them off as we went. The stadiums were big markers. It was always great to reach a club, to tick another one off and to pause for a moment, take a photograph, maybe do an interview, and to get some food and drink.

It was great to return to stadiums where I played, such as Old Trafford or Anfield, and to visit the new ones, built since I retired, such as the Etihad or the Emirates. The team enjoyed it, too. There is something special about being pitch-side at these stadiums, even if it can be surreal with no fans inside.

The accents changed as we moved around the country. I met so many people and enjoyed new conversations on subjects I never thought I would be discussing. All these things helped me to break up the daily routine.

I tried to attack it and enjoy it. I tried to enjoy the company and it always generated a PR buzz when one of the current players from the Premier League or the Championship came out in support. Drew Surman, an ex-Saint and local Southampton boy was playing for Bournemouth at the time so he came to see us off at the very start, and there were many others along the way.

I was running down a country lane outside Derby when I became aware of a large, four-wheel drive vehicle crawling alongside me. I turned my head to see what this driver was playing at, just as the windows came down. Everyone inside shouted and cheered and Kelvin Davis, the former Saints goalkeeper, popped his head out, grinned and said something like, 'Fancy seeing you here.' Kelvin had brought the whole family along, and we all stopped for a brief chat and they followed us for the rest of the day.

Steve Davis, one of my old teammates in the Saints youth team and a Burnley legend, joined me as I ran into Turf Moor, although the steep climb away from the ground and straight up into the Pennines on the bike was one of the most difficult rides of the fortnight. I was up and out of my saddle the whole time, moving slowly, zigzagging to avoid grinding to a complete halt with my feet clipped into my pedals and falling over.

Every show of support helped to keep us going. We had a great group on the road, but the days were so long, and sometimes monotonous, that simply having a new face around really uplifted the mood in camp. A friend called Liam Edgar turned up on the day we lost Ian to a mechanical fault and managed to give everyone a boost, adopting Deano's role as the joker in the team, with his impersonations and silly walks. Liam serenading the hotel staff with his version of the Righteous Brothers' classic 'You've Lost That Loving Feeling' at the end of another long day has lived long in the memory of those who witnessed it.

* * *

Time spent thinking of others often made me emotional. Those were the occasions when I would just burst into tears, as on the first challenge. On one stretch on the road between Hull and Leeds, I was thinking of our close friend Vicky and her cancer diagnosis.

She had a young family, three beautiful girls, and she had so much to live for. They thought she might have gallstones when she went for tests, only to find out it was cancer, which started in her colon and spread to her bowel. The diagnosis was serious.

Vicky was one of our biggest supporters through the challenges and, sadly, died in October 2019, a couple of months after her 50th birthday. We will never forget her, or the help she and her family gave us.

There were times when the strength of these feelings drove me on and other times when I simply had to close down my emotions and empty my mind. I would shut off the emotion to shut out the pain. Think of absolutely nothing. Try to go numb. Just keep putting one foot in front of the other. Keep pedalling. Concentrate on the rhythm.

The Fitbit on my wrist was the only thing I would focus any attention on. I liked to break the day into blocks of 10 miles and the device would alert me when I covered a mile, always eating away at the big number.

Leaving Norwich, after that terrible night of excruciating pain, was one of the longest distances we faced, with the marathon and more than 100 miles on the bike. I was taking painkillers constantly but they did little more than take the edge off the pain as we went into Ipswich and turned back towards London.

We were nearly at Tottenham by the close of the day. Andrew was riding with me, along with a couple of my friends, Wayne and Miles. They had come to join the cycling but found me in such low spirits they rode beside me through the marathon as well to offer moral support. The four of us were riding through Epping Forest. It was getting dark and we had been going for so long in terrible conditions that the lights were starting to fail on our bikes.

We had one working front light between us and one working rear light. We had to position ourselves with the working front light at the front of our group and the working rear light at the back. On public roads with heavy traffic that was a bit hairy.

Earlier in the challenge, after leaving Stoke City, the team took me off the road because it was becoming dangerous. It was dusk and I was cycling alone on a dual carriageway where it was busy with lorries. I was tiring and it wasn't a good situation from a safety perspective. One of the support vehicles was crawling along slowly behind me and we were causing a small degree of chaos on the road.

We were not far short of the mileage and I agreed to call an early finish to the day as long as we made up the difference, which we did, adding a few miles here and there.

On average, each marathon was taking me up to five hours to complete. On the bike, I was travelling at an average of around 14 mph, which worked out at up to seven hours of cycling once we took pit stops for food and drink into account. Once again, the days were long. We used the ice baths again and found very little time for rest and recovery.

The variety of the two disciplines helped though. If I was struggling on the run, I could look forward to climbing onto the bike, even if I never felt 100 per cent safe when cycling. There were no falls but there was always a genuine element of uncertainty in my mind, even with all those miles under my belt. I knew I had to stay totally focused to stay safe.

* * *

When we reached Tottenham, I felt as though the worst was behind us. London would be intense, as we knew from the first challenge. There were many clubs to cram in so lots of stopping and starting. Timings and navigation was difficult and the traffic in the capital meant it was more trouble for the team in the vehicles than for me on foot or on the bike.

Personally, I liked the buzz of hitting lots of clubs in quick succession, ticking them off in my mind. There was more media coverage and things to see and capture my imagination.

Gary Mabbutt came to greet us again at Spurs, and we made it through the city to Brentford where I transitioned to the bike and cycled to Watford, then Reading – our finishing point.

The day dragged on because of the number of stops and the traffic congestion. The team were not always able to stay with me and there were times when I had to pause on the bike ride to find out which way we were supposed to go. There was a puncture and an issue with a bracket on my light, which I had to fix with tape.

All of these things meant we were late into Reading where, unbeknown to me, there was quite a welcome, including the families and supporters and three Saints players Kelvin Davis, Shane Long and Steven Davis. I was taken aback by the size of the crowd. It was the biggest since the start and reinforced the feeling that I was getting closer to home. My first thought was, 'Oh no, how long have they all been waiting?'

Sir John Madejski, the former owner and chairman of Reading FC and an honorary life-president, welcomed us to his club and he was wonderful. He literally had the keys to the Madejski Stadium in his hand and said, 'Come inside and do whatever you need to do.' We posed for lots of photos including a huge group photograph of everyone who was there. We did some interviews before Sir John locked up very late at night.

On the penultimate day, we finished at Brighton's Amex Stadium as they were playing against Preston North End in the Championship. We arrived as the match was ending and Preston had scored a last-minute equaliser but Brighton manager Chris Hughton insisted we had full access to the dressing rooms and all the facilities we needed. It is a testament to the type of man Chris is, he probably wasn't feeling great about losing two points at the end of the game but he was determined to do all he could for us that night.

The football family were firmly behind us and some clubs went out of their way to help. Preston were also superb when we were up at Deepdale, and one of their physios joined us for the day on his bike.

The final day was a marathon out of Brighton. I was joined once again by the Saints chairman at the time, Ralph Krueger, and another ex-Southampton left-back, Dan Harding.

There was a shorter bike ride to the Ageas Bowl, home of Hampshire County Cricket Club, on the outskirts of Southampton, where our friend and club chairman Rod Bransgrove gave us access to the home dressing room as I changed back into my running kit.

There was a big group of us for this final stage of the challenge, a run across the city to St Mary's, where Saints were playing against Burnley. The pain seemed to disperse amid the excitement, knowing we were going to reach the finishing line.

It was an incredible feeling to be back again, second time around. People lined the streets and quite literally threw money at us. They were turning out their pockets and throwing it into the cars through the open windows. The footwell of Karen's car was full of cash. Andrew got back onto his bike and rode alongside us with a bucket and the crowds filled it up with money.

The scenes at the stadium honestly reminded me of the famous running scene from Rocky II, where he sets out on a training run, waving to a few people as they shout his name and, by the end, there are hundreds following him as he races across the park, up the steps and leaps into the air.

We found hundreds of supporters and friends waiting on the road leading to St Mary's and they all joined us as we ran to the stadium.

Inside the ground, thousands of Southampton fans were waiting to roar us home at half time and they made a noise as though Saints had scored. The Big Race volunteers had printed 32,000 Benali masks and fixed one to every seat with the permission of the club. Supporters pulled them on as I came in and completed a lap of the pitch. It was rather strange to glance up into the crowd and see thousands of people with my face looking back at me.

I was jogging towards the finish line when Paul Watts, our team photographer, slipped over in front of me as he tried to get a picture and nearly wiped me out, bringing an ironic cheer from the fans. That would have been amusing, to cover more than 1,400 miles, only to be taken out by one of the team within a few feet of the finish.

Happiness, pride and relief, all tangled up inside my head. As if all of this wasn't enough, Kenzie had recently become Southampton's pitch-side presenter. She was waiting with the microphone at the finish line. She was emotional too, and it made for a lovely interview. We both knew what a physical and mental rollercoaster the last two weeks had been and here we were, at the end. Another challenge completed. It felt like a genuine accomplishment.

10

IRON FRAN

'It was the end of August 2018 when the text message came from Franny, wishing us well and asking for a chat. I knew what this meant and there were two options. Option One was to bury my phone, eat my SIM card and lie low for a few months. Option Two was to rejoin the team after the disappointment of missing the second challenge and help him out.

It was sure to be another bonkers idea, pushing him to the very limit of what should be mentally and physically possible, even for the most able and determined human. "OK, whatever it is, I'm in," I told him. We met in November. "Iron Fran", he told me, was going to be an Iron Man Triathlon every day for a whole week, starting in April.

People train for years to do just one Iron Man. Franny was just starting out, he was planning to do seven in seven days and, by his own admission, he was not even a very good swimmer. Maybe I should have taken Option One.'

Dean Cartledge, Iron Fran route manager

We were sunbathing on the top deck of a cruise liner in the Mediterranean Sea when I told Karen that for the third challenge I was thinking of running until I literally dropped. 'What a stupid idea,' she replied. 'As if we're all going to stand around until you actually collapse and then all cheer because that's the challenge completed.' When she put it like that I could see what she meant. We were on the P&O *Ventura*. I was on board as a guest speaker and throwing around ideas about where to go with the next challenge.

I was still chasing the million pounds and my mind was set on going again. We were up to £665,000 when all the fundraising events for the Big Race were over. I still wanted to reach seven figures and was encouraged and delighted by the reaction to what we had achieved so far.

I received an honorary degree from Solent University, making me a doctor of sport for services to the local community, and the Freedom of the City from Southampton City Council. It was nice to be recognised in this way and very flattering. That wasn't the reason I was doing this but it was reassuring to know our challenges were capturing the public imagination as well as raising money for a good cause. I did not intend to stop now. I was determined to push on and reach my target. It was just a question of what to do next.

Swimming the Channel was another idea I toyed with. Running the Tour de France was another. On closer inspection, the Tour is a route more than 2,000 miles long and, once the reality of the mountain stages dawned on me, that didn't seem so wise. Do we take it overseas? I was Googling away again. Do we stick with the football theme? Or will people think, 'Oh, he's done that before.'

I wanted to keep people engaged. If we were asking for more donations, then it would have to be bigger and harder than the previous two. Equally, we had done a three-week and a two-week challenge, and this was a huge demand on the volunteers who give up their time and take holiday from work to be on the support team.

Karen and I agreed we should make sure it covered a shorter time span. She suggested a 24-hour challenge, before we settled on a week. And we moved away from the football theme. Stopping at the clubs stretched the days out, and that proved to be a bit of a problem on the second challenge because there were 44 to visit. London was the most notable. The clubs were very accommodating and, whenever we dropped in, we felt a certain responsibility to spend time there. It would be rude to simply turn up, tick them off, take a picture and dash off again.

The Big Run had been all running, one discipline over three weeks. The Big Race was two weeks and we added the bike, a second discipline. It seemed a natural progression to add a third discipline and come down to one week. We decided on the Iron Man Triathlon, which was the ultimate three-discipline challenge: a 2.4-mile swim, a 112-mile bike ride and then a marathon.

To push the boundaries I decided to go for seven in seven days. Karen came up with the name 'Iron Fran', which had a nice ring to it. That's how the third challenge was sealed while flat out on a sunbed, sailing around beneath the clear blue skies. We were quite chuffed with our idea, and Karen was pleased she could go back to reading her book.

* * *

Perhaps the sunshine and the holiday vibe led me to be a little blasé about the swimming. 'Oh yeah, and this time we'll throw in some swimming,' as if that would be no trouble. I knew how to swim, I figured. I swam in the pool when we were on holiday and so I assumed that as long as I put in the hours of training I would reach the distance required. This confidence turned out to be badly misplaced.

Back home, I turned for help to Lucy Williams, an instructor we knew because she taught Luke and Kenzie. She had also competed at international level and coached triathletes. My first question for her was, 'Have I left this too late?' She had never seen me swim so she invited me to the pool and told me to swim a length. She watched carefully and then said, 'Right, we'll have to change everything.'

Swimming is all about the technique. That was her point. 'You're not going to muscle it out,' she said. 'This is not about being super-fit. I know you can do ultra-running and cycling but in the pool that will get you nowhere. We have to strip back your stroke and learn properly.'

To reach the required distance, and still have energy left to complete the other two elements of the triathlon she told me we would have to start from scratch. To hammer the point home, Lucy told me an Olympic legend like Michael Phelps would cover the length of this 25-metre pool with just a handful of strokes. For any competitive swimmer it would be about a dozen. It had just taken me more than 40.

This just went to show how uneconomical my technique was. I was splashing around, using loads of energy without really going anywhere. And this was the end of November and we were planning to start the challenge at the end of April. We had less than five months to build me into a swimmer who could cover 156 lengths each day for seven days. At the moment, I could not swim 10 metres (33 feet) to Lucy's satisfaction. 'This won't be easy,' she promised, and she was right, but if she thought I was a hopeless case, she didn't let on. She asked me to put my faith in her, and I did. What I lacked in technique, I made up for in determination.

We started lessons and I gave it everything. Three or four times a week, I was in the water at 6 a.m. and we spent months going over a series of technical drills. I swam in fins to focus on the position of my head, and with floats to work on my legs, and loosening up what she called my stiff 'footballers' ankles'.

One of the exercises seemed to be something like a doggy paddle. Another time, I was doing the backstroke to use different muscles. We even did a short session on competition-style tumble turns, but only one. We swiftly abandoned it and worked on simpler touch turns.

I trusted Lucy. I knew I wasn't a very good swimmer but as the weeks ticked by I thought I really ought to be doing 30 or 40 lengths and crashing some longer distances out. Lucy, in contrast, did not seem bothered about the distance. She would keep telling me I had to 'catch' the water and talked about what swimmers call 'feel'. This went on for months and I was still unable to grasp what she was asking me to do.

It was all so alien. I started to come home in a panic after a session in the pool because I had only managed to swim for two lengths consecutively and the challenge was looming when I was planning to swim for 2.4 miles per day.

Ten weeks prior to the start and I was still struggling. I recorded a short video message on my phone to document the problems I was having, gulping down water, working too hard, my legs were sinking all the time. I was even waking up with a head full of cold symptoms because I was taking in so much chlorine.

There was still so much to work on. Unbeknown to me at the time, Lucy was also quietly concerned. She confided in Andrew, my cycling partner, that his six-year-old daughter Isla, who she also taught, had a better technique than I did. This was only a few weeks before the start.

Fortunately, she was not quite so blunt when talking to me. That would have deflated my morale. Instead, she was incredibly patient. She would tell me not to worry about the endurance, that something will click and it will feel right, and that my technique will come together and I will start catching the water.

She was right – the Eureka moment did arrive. Not in the sense that I was transformed overnight into an Olympic swimmer but there was a click and a point where it made sense. I knew what she had been trying to get me to understand.

It came together in the last month and that coincided with us stepping up the distance. I found my rhythm. Quite a lot of swimmers breathe every four strokes. That's what I started out trying to do but it just wasn't right.

Instead, I settled into a breathing pattern every two strokes. I would do one length breathing to my left and the next length breathing on my right, to avoid turning my neck only in one direction. If I was to make the distance, I had to relax my mind and lose the tension from my upper shoulders and neck. At the start of the training programme, we set a target of 32 strokes per length. We got it down to 26 and then we really started to build up the distances.

One day Lucy asked to join me on the challenge and I did not hesitate to say yes. Until then, I had been expecting to do the swims on my own. We had done a number of sessions together and I took confidence from swimming with her, in the way I did from cycling with Andrew.

She knew me as a swimmer. She was able to give me tips on my pace and might give me a signal to slow down or remind me about techniques such as gliding into the turn, rather than using another stroke.

* * *

It was great to have her on board, and the team was growing. The whole event seemed to be bigger than the previous two challenges. Deano was keen to be part of it after missing the Big Race. He designed a route that started in Manchester on 29 April, 2019. We would zig-zag south across the country and reach Southampton one week later, to coincide with the Southampton Marathon, before cycling a route around the New Forest and back to a finish line at Guildhall Square.

Kelly was in again and Ian was keen to help, although a health scare meant he wasn't able to ride his motorbike. Nicole Vickery, a close family friend, accepted the role as our project manager, Tom Lay from Cancer Research UK joined us, and Andrew promised to ride every mile with me, which was a big commitment because the cycling mileage was quite a bit further than in the Big Race.

Seven Iron Man triathlons would be a total of 784 miles on the bike but, as we were not part of any official competition, we always

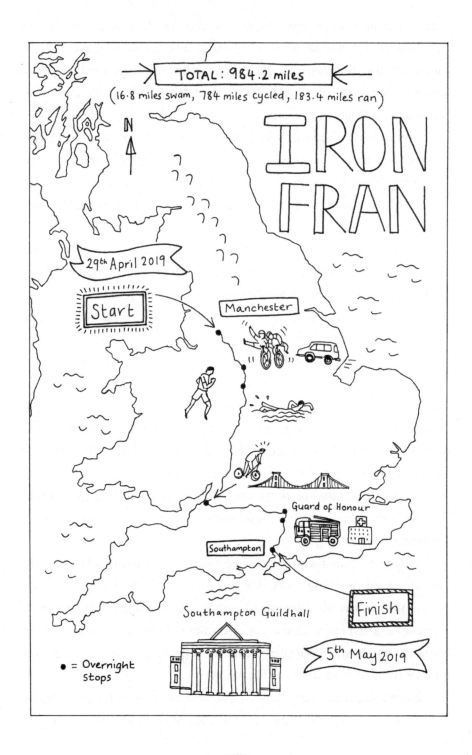

erred on the side of caution, measuring too far rather than not far enough. I did not want to cheat the challenge and those making donations by shaving miles off, even accidentally, so our cycling routes were set for us to ride about 115 miles each day rather than the official distance of 112.

Only once on the Big Race, the previous challenge, did we top 100 miles in a single day on the bikes and, although Andrew was an experienced cyclist, he had never ridden further than 300 miles in a week. There was some serious training ahead for both of us. My bike had been in the garage for months. I dragged it out and dusted away the cobwebs but training on the bikes proved difficult in the wet and windy conditions we experienced in the early months of 2019. Training on the bike amounted to somewhere between five and 10 hours a week. Often closer to five hours than 10. I was doing some form of training every day but concentrating chiefly on the swimming.

Andrew dragged me out for one training ride of more than 100 miles but that was it. We went out into the New Forest on another occasion and found the paths blocked by fallen trees. The fire brigade were out chopping one of them up as we climbed over it with our bikes. We had not once covered the required distance of 112 miles before Iron Fran started.

My preparations for the run were even worse. I had developed a soreness in a calf muscle and it stopped me from running. I felt it niggling away during an 11-mile training run. I rested it for a few weeks and tried to focus on improving my fitness and stamina through the swimming and cycling.

Running was my strongest discipline. I knew I could run. I wasn't unduly worried about that until I came to start again. Less than a mile into my first run, I could feel it pulling. I thought back to my playing days when I had similar niggles and I was afraid the muscle was about to go any second. I had to stop.

I limped back home feeling dejected. It was painful and I was cursing my luck. I went into the first challenge with a knee problem. On the second one, I felt good going into it, only to be troubled by hamstring and Achilles tendon injuries all the way round. I wanted to go into this third challenge bang on it, feeling fit and with all the training under my belt. Unfortunately, that was not going to be possible.

I went to have the calf injury checked out by the medical team at Southampton FC. They arranged a scan, which confirmed a tear, and said to have any chance of doing this challenge on the allotted dates you cannot go running. They gave me some exercises and said it was fine to carrying on swimming and cycling, which I did.

It was now only three weeks before the start and still I had not done a training run of more than 11 miles. I simply did not have the mileage in the tank to be thinking about running a marathon. I knew from experience this was going to mess with my head. I needed to run so I went out and did a 14-miler, more for my own peace of mind than anything else. I was blowing a bit. My body was not in the habit of running this distance but at least the calf seemed to have healed, and that was a big relief.

* * *

We had three main sponsors backing this challenge: Southern Communications, who had been the main sponsors of the Big Race were back on board, together with Fitbit and The Hendy Group. We had a convoy of vehicles, the Iron Fran van, and three cars donated by Hendy. We even had a motorhome, kindly provided by a local company called Webbs, which proved invaluable.

The motorhome served as Nicole's mobile office. She spent about 18 hours a day in there. It also gave us somewhere to store the equipment in one place, and somewhere to change kit between the disciplines rather than in the back of a car. It also came with an in-built fridge and a freezer, which enabled us to store the fresh and healthy food supplied by Southampton FC, who offered great support once again. Saints chef Angus Dunlop created an amazing menu of food, with shrink-wrapped meals, soups and snacks to take with us and heat up or cook as we went along.

We collected the bulk of it on Sunday morning as we set off to Manchester (Karen and I flew whilst the rest of the team drove the vehicles up to keep me rested and more relaxed). There seemed to be enough to feed an army. Then they came out and dropped a fresh supply with us when we were back in the south, later in the week.

Ian slept in the motorhome to guard the precious cargo and Stu Amey drove it from point to point. Stu had worked on the previous challenges as an employee of Cancer Research UK but was not working on this particular one, so he took a week off and joined the team. It summed up the attitude of so many.

We all loved having him around and we remember him giving an incredible speech at the gala dinner after the second challenge, the Big Race, when he told the story of his wife Michelle who, at the age of 31, was diagnosed with an advanced melanoma. Michelle, he explained, decided early on in her treatment that she didn't like to hear directly from the doctors when they reported the results of her various scans and clinical trials. Stu began to do this for her and, after one of the very early clinical trials, he came out of a consultation with advice to go home and enjoy Christmas because it would be Michelle's last. How do you go home and pass on that news to your wife and young children?

His speech went on, everyone hanging on his every word as he told how, now, more than 10 years later, they were going through more clinical trials and Michelle was still fighting. There wasn't a dry eye in the room. Then, he said, 'And Michelle is here with me tonight,' and they panned the camera to her. She looked beautiful. It was such a powerfully charged moment. We all thought Stu was standing up to say a few words about the challenge and out came one of the most compelling speeches I have ever heard. It was the perfect reminder of why we were all engaged in this process.

* * *

To rewind a little: Karen's mum, Eileen, passed away suddenly in October 2017. This wasn't connected to cancer. She went into hospital for what we expected to be a routine procedure and we lost her. It was a terrible shock and an incredibly painful time for us all.

Everyone loved Eileen. She had always been at the heart of our family and I shared a very close and special relationship with her. She and Bill embraced me from day one as the son they had never had and the depth of feeling was mutual, I could not have loved them more.

Although she had very little interest in football, Eileen often came to cheer me on when I played, and could get herself quite worked up when she was in the stands. Her blood pressure once shot up to such a degree it gave her a nosebleed. My antics probably didn't help. The only away game she ever came to see was at Tottenham when I received a red card for a high tackle on Nicky Barmby.

When it came to the endurance challenges, Eileen always worried about me. Whenever she called to check how I was, Karen would say, 'Oh, don't worry Mum, you know what he's like, he has an angel on his shoulder.'

The Iron Fran kits were already designed and had been sent for manufacturing when Karen came up with the idea to embroider a small pair of angel wings on the shoulders of the shirts in memory of her mum. I thought it was a brilliant suggestion. We called the manufacturers and made the necessary alterations.

It was a perfect tribute and angel wings became the symbol of the third challenge. It was a symbol for everyone who had lost someone close to them and when Karen saw me running or cycling, she could see the wings embroidered on the shoulder of my shirt and take some comfort.

She would say her mum was looking out for me and that certainly seemed to be the case when we flirted with disaster, early in the bike ride on the very first morning. Andrew was out in front and I was locked onto his rear wheel as we flew along, travelling downhill on a three-lane carriageway with traffic lights ahead. When they turned green in our favour, Andrew kept up the speed. We were moving at about 40 mph and covering ground quickly.

My first realisation that something was wrong was when he suddenly veered off course. A car had jumped the lights at the junction and turned across our path. The driver must have failed to see us. I hit the brakes but there was no way we could stop in time. My back wheel locked and skidded.

Andrew had a split second to decide whether to take us to the left or right. If the driver saw us and stopped, going left was the right decision. If the driver carried on, going left would mean a certain crash. Andrew went left and I followed. Luckily, the driver spotted us at the last moment and stopped the car in mid-turn.

I will never know how but somehow I avoided any impact with Andrew's bike or the car. It certainly wasn't because I knew what I was doing. It was purely a reflex reaction. I followed Andrew and we both emerged on the other side still on two wheels. My heart was beating fast. We looked at each other. Then we looked back.

Gary Platt was also riding with us. His wife Di worked for Cancer Research UK when I started my challenges and, although she had since moved to another job, they both joined us to support this challenge. Gary was also through the scrape in one piece. Everyone stayed on their wheels. When we pulled alongside each other we all said, 'What on earth happened there?' or words to that effect. It felt as if those angel wings were helping and Eileen, my number one fan, was right there on my shoulder.

* * *

The initial plan had been to take in a few football grounds and Cancer Research UK shops along the way but the time constraints made it impossible. On average, an Iron Man triathlete will take 13 hours to complete the event and we had added complications.

Parts of the route were dictated by a deal we struck with the David Lloyd Leisure group to use their swimming facilities. We were in pools rather than open water for both safety and logistical reasons. With the changing in between, and stopping for food breaks, I was taking 16 to 17 hours to complete each Iron Man.

The proposed timeframes were: Up at 4.50 a.m. for breakfast and physio, leave the hotel at 5.45, swim at 6, cycle from about 8.40 a.m. to 5.20 p.m., start the marathon at 5.40 p.m., finish around 10.40 and be tucked up in the marshmallow bed after an ice bath, food and physio by 11.20. There was not a lot of wriggle room.

Nicole selected hotels close to the pools. We needed to be in the water before they were open to the public and we were asking someone to get out of bed, open up early and rope off a designated lane for our private use. We could not have done the challenge without all these small acts of kindness.

Lucy was a positive force and it was reassuring to have her in the water alongside me. The 2.4-mile swim took us about an hour-and-a-half. I would swim 40 or 50 lengths and then pause to eat a yoghurt or a Muller Rice and take in fluids. Nutrition was going to be very important.

With the help of Cancer Research UK, we had names of people affected by cancer on my swim cap. Some of them would come and support me while I was in the pool and I would dedicate that part of the triathlon to them each morning. This never failed to provide extra motivation as I climbed on the bike and set off on the long ride towards our next destination. Similarly, I had the names of Vicky Chappell and Michelle Amey printed on two of my running shirts, a personal touch for two lovely friends.

* * *

Kenzie ran 15 miles of the marathon with me in Nottingham at the end of the first day. It was hilly and my muscles were screaming but I made it to the end. Deano devoted lots of time to planning and driving the routes in advance to ensure it was as safe as possible. He thought, in hindsight, we ought to have stayed out of the cities to use straighter and flatter routes but so much of the running was done in the dark that it helped to have the street lighting of the cities.

Every element of the day was like a military operation. There were the usual ice baths and physio sessions to aid recovery. Sleep was scarce. I was sleeping for only between four and five hours a night. Some of the team slept even less.

I was back in my trusty marshmallow bed. One night I climbed in, fell asleep in an instant and, in what seemed like five minutes, it was time to wake up. It was a good, solid sleep but it didn't seem anywhere near long enough. Most nights though were broken and uncomfortable, with extreme fatigue in my legs.

Then there were occasional curve balls thrown in, maybe me struggling and moving too slowly or taking too long to change kit between the disciplines. We had to be quick on our feet to move with the problems as they came up.

* * *

There were some comical moments, too. The second day was a flattish cycling route, heading east from Nottingham towards the Wash and doubling back towards Leicester. According to my Fitbit we were a few yards short of the 26.2 miles as we finished the run. I turned into the hotel car park and the staff were there to form a welcome party together, along with the whole support team and a few guests from the hotel. They burst into applause and must have wondered what I was up to as I veered off down a pathway to run behind the hotel and do a few laps of the car park to get my mileage up to the 26.2 mark.

Our peloton had grown quite large by the time we took on the long bike ride from Leicester to Bristol. Lots of friends and supporters joined us, and this made it tough for Deano in the lead car. We didn't want him disappearing too far into the distance. Nor did we want him crawling along too slowly with cyclists overtaking him or crashing into the back of his vehicle.

As on the first challenge, the Big Run, my single biggest problem was consuming the 10,500 calories I needed to keep me going. I did not have much of an appetite all week. Kelly handed me food and drink from the moment I woke up. There would be a breakfast shake to force down, protein-packed pancakes and muesli bars.

When I look back at the meals served up to me on Iron Fran, they sound delicious. Saints chef Angus conjured up dishes such as king prawns with chorizo and lentils, or steamed salmon with asparagus and lemon and dill sauce. I am a big foodie and this is exactly the sort of food I would order in a restaurant but I found it impossible to consume it in the necessary quantities.

I knew from experience I could not plough through large platefuls in the middle of a challenge. I would be pushing food around my plate with Karen and the kids or Kelly or Nicole trying to persuade me to eat just another forkful. Every meal came with the sort of negotiation process you might have with a child when you explain there will not be any ice cream unless you eat at least so much of the main course.

As the week went on, they started to puree the food and Angus supplied more high-calorie smoothies because he figured they would be easier and quicker to get down.

Someone was always passing me something to eat – bananas, energy bars, brownies, trail mix and even baby food – but eating while cycling can be tricky. I would be pouring it all over myself, and there were times when Andrew was actually stuffing morsels of food into my mouth as we rode along. Even when I did manage to get a few mouthfuls down, the intense level of exercise meant I was regurgitating. This did nothing to encourage my appetite. Sometimes I would take a sandwich or a slice of malt loaf from someone and sneakily deposit it in the nearest bush when I thought nobody was looking.

* * *

The run into Bristol on Day Three was where things started to go more seriously wrong. We ended with a steep climb near the Clifton Suspension Bridge and I began to notice something other than the obvious aches and pains.

I can remember lying in my marshmallow bed at the Travelodge at Cribbs Causeway, folding my arms across my chest and my heart was racing as if I was doing heavy exercise. I was resting and my heart was beating like a drum. I was concerned. I knew it was not normal, but I kept it to myself and thought I would get a good night's rest and see how it was in the morning.

Any Iron Man is a huge struggle but Day Four proved to be absolutely brutal. Although the swim went OK, the bike was just a massive grind, up and over the Clifton Bridge. It was tediously slow going through the hills and then turning east, roughly parallel with the M4.

I was very quiet on the bike. I didn't want to chat with the support team. The long stretch towards Reading wasn't the most demanding but Andrew said I was like a dead man riding. I was withdrawing into myself. The lights were going out. I spent most of the ride looking down at the floor or fixed my eyes on the back wheel of Andrew's bike.

About five miles before the end of the ride and the changeover to running at Reading RUFC, the heavens opened and we suffered a real soaking in a torrential downpour. I was feeling tired and it was starting to show. I tried to get some food down.

We were drenched to the skin and, as soon as we were out running on the main road, some heavy lorries roared through puddles only a few feet away to give us another soaking and add to the misery. The support vehicles lost us, cut off by roadworks on a bridge to the frustration of Kelly who was growing concerned by my condition. I just wasn't in a good place physically or mentally. My vision was blurred and I was unable to read the display on my Fitbit device. It was taking a monumental effort just to lift my feet up onto the kerb. My mood was darkening, and the rain was still hammering down around me.

I put my earphones in and shut everyone off including the two lads from the local running club who had kindly come to run with me. Deano politely explained I was in no shape for conversation and best left to my own devices, and that they were in fact really helping my morale just by being there and running alongside me. That was true. I do hope they weren't offended.

The rain eased at around 8 miles and my support caught up again so we had a short stop for dry kit. Kelly asked if I was feeling alright. She had noticed me weaving around and making strange decisions, running out of my way to find a dropped kerb to avoid stepping up onto the pavements. I told her I was struggling, which was not an admission I would normally make, but that I had no intention of stopping.

I flicked anxiously at the rubber charity band on my right wrist. During preparations for each of the three challenges, I had sessions with a transformational coach called Donna Bache, in Winchester. She used a blend of techniques including hypnosis, subliminal messaging and visualisation, all designed to help endurance. During the sessions, I was almost asleep. In a trance, perhaps. But I did find it helped me understand ways to alter my state of mind and thought process. Tying the laces on my trainers invigorated my day and the ice bath was the start of body-healing time. The flick of the wristband was supposed to be a trigger to help me push through the toughest times. Overall, it was a big help. Except this time, it didn't seem to matter what I did.

I trudged through to the end. There were quite a few people running with me, one of them had done the whole marathon. Deano ran with me for the last few miles, wearing a headlamp because it was pitch black. It was gone 10 p.m. by the time we finished. There was a strong welcome committee at the Holiday Inn, in Farnborough, with friends from Southampton. Nicole had arranged for the local fire brigade, three trucks with their lights flashing, to form a guard of honour.

I tried to give them a smile and say thank you but I could not face any extended pleasantries. I was staggering, losing my balance and my vision was failing. The team knew something was wrong beyond simple fatigue. I went straight inside, took an ice bath, a shower and had some physio.

Kelly and Nicole cleared everyone out of the room quickly so I could try to eat and have as much rest as possible. I climbed into my marshmallow bed and literally did not move. The day had been relentless and I was utterly exhausted. I was unable to eat anything. My heart was thumping again. I knew something was wrong.

I was not in any excruciating pain, not the way I was on the second challenge in Norwich. Instead, I had an overall feeling of dread. I was worried about my heart. I knew it was not normal for it to be beating so quickly when I was at rest.

Losing my vision felt weird. I was starting to fear what I might be doing to my body. Was it shutting down? Had I reached a breaking point? These things were going wrong and there were still three days to go. I set my alarm for four in the morning.

Karen was naturally very anxious. There were quite a few worries for her to choose from but, weeks later, she looked back and identified that night as the worst of them, across all three challenges.

It was about 1.30 a.m. when I asked her to put a hand on my chest to feel my heart pounding. She thought it was beating abnormally. It felt as though it was going to come out of my chest. We called Kelly, who didn't answer, and we didn't know her room number. We could have found out but Kelly needed to sleep, too. Besides, she would be coming into our room soon enough to prepare for Day Five.

When she came in, just after 4 a.m., I told her I had had the same issue with my heartbeat the previous night. This came as a shock to Karen, who wanted to know why I declined to mention it at the time. Within half an hour, Kelly had withdrawn me from the challenge on medical grounds.

She launched into a heartfelt speech to tell me how much all the team cared about me, that they all understood how badly I wanted to carry on, and that it was the last thing she wanted to do, but that my health had to come first.

I was still in my bed. I listened to her speech and nodded in agreement and then, when she had finished, I said, 'So shall I get back in the pool and give it a go?' Kelly shot me a look of utter disbelief, like, 'Are you for real?'

I don't remember this conversation. In fact, I don't remember very much at all from this early morning exchange but we have it all on film and it's clear I was behaving completely irrationally. Karen is convinced I was delirious, and she and Kelly knew I was devastated to be withdrawn from the challenge.

Kelly called Dr Drew Rakhit, a consultant cardiologist at Southampton General Hospital, who had run a series of tests on me before this challenge got under way to make sure my cardiovascular system was in good condition. Drew ordered me to come in straight away. We borrowed a car from a team member. We thought it might attract attention if we drove one of the Iron Fran branded cars up to the doors of the accident and emergency unit.

As I left for the hospital that morning, Nicole got everyone out of bed for a team meeting and informed them of my withdrawal. They unanimously agreed that they would hold the fort and continue the challenge in my absence. We had no idea how the public would react to this. We didn't know if they would lose interest. In fact, we soon found out people threw their support more firmly behind us when they realised I had put my health at risk.

Everyone played a part without question. Lucy was my champion in the pool. Andrew on the bike, with Gary and others. That evening, the running group swelled until it was about 20 strong. I don't know where they all came from. Luke went out and ran the first 20 miles. I think it helped take his mind away from worrying about me.

At the hospital, they had a bed waiting and an intravenous drip at the ready. They wired me up and scanned my heart. They took blood and urine samples. Drew gave us a matter-of-fact talk about what he expected to find.

One of his serious fears was a condition called rhabdomyolysis, a condition where extreme exercise can cause muscle fibres to break down and pass into the bloodstream. It can cause kidney failure and have fatal consequences if untreated.

In that private room with Karen, Kelly and Luke, surrounded by all the medical machinery as we waited for the specialists to return with more test results, I was utterly despondent. Luke was afraid the doctor was going to return and tell him his dad had permanently damaged his heart. It was horrendous. I was concerned too and hoped there was no serious damage, but my overriding thought was that I should be out in the pool, on the bike and running.

The first test results came back. Fortunately, they were all clear and, as Drew was talking to me, explaining there were still other results to come back, there was a knock on the door and someone else came into the room to say another set of results were absolutely fine. People kept popping in and out like a scene from a hospital drama. Within an hour, all the tests were back and the results were normal.

Drew was amazed. I had seen him for the tests ahead of Iron Fran and he was aware of the disruption to my training regime, and he knew my attention to diet had not been quite what it should have been. He had seemed shocked to find I was still feasting on the odd KFC. He also noted that, although I was in reasonably good shape and more accustomed to endurance sport than before, the fitness results at the start of Iron Fran had not been as strong as they were before the first two challenges.

Overall, Drew thought my body had coped well with the first four days of the challenge but he still recommended 48 hours of complete rest. My body had reached its maximum, he said. The tests might be clear but to ignore the signs would be to invite my body to crash again and risk long-term damage to my vital organs. He knew how much it meant to me to finish the challenge and said that if I went away and had 48 hours of complete rest, that would give me a chance to take in some food, rehydrate and complete the last day.

The next day, Day Six, I got in the pool.

11

ONE MILLION

'Fran has some kind of invincible human strength within him. This, I am sure of. I know how that may sound, but I am constantly bowled over by his mental toughness and resilience. I've seen him pushing his body through pain barriers very few people could go through. I know I couldn't do the things he's done. I could barely run a mile. What he has inside of him is special. I believe he can do anything he says he's going to do.

When someone told me he couldn't possibly do seven Iron Man triathlons in seven days I thought, "Yes, he can, Fran can do it," even though he'd never done one in his life. I've seen him go to hell and back and still keep going. I've watched him crawl across the floor in the middle of the night because he cannot bear to put his body weight on his foot and then get up the next day and run a marathon and cycle more than 100 miles.

I never wanted him to do any of these things. I'm his wife, and his health will always be my number one concern. But Fran wanted to use his inner strength for good. It's something that has been imbedded within him since he was young. He had it as a footballer and everyone could see it. It has driven him through these challenges and when we were in the hospital and all the tests came back, the cardiologist told me that the best way to describe it from a medical point of view was simply that he's not human.

I didn't need a cardiologist to tell me what I have known since the day I met him, my husband has a heart of gold.'

Karen Benali, Franny's wife

I wasn't trying to be a hero by ignoring the medical advice. I sat and listened to everything and it made perfect sense. I went against it because the idea of completing the challenge consumed me. It was like a form of tunnel vision.

I was so desperately disappointed to have missed Day Five that it seemed like the only thing that mattered. I can see how the extreme endurance athletes slip easily into a danger zone when not looking through clear eyes.

My family were very worried. Kelly, Drew and the specialists at Southampton General were all saying it was time to stop. I believed them when they said I was at breaking point. Yet I got up on Day Six and really wanted to get in the water and give it a go.

I figured missing one day was better than missing two. Kelly was not comfortable with this at all. Nor was Karen. There is nobody who cares more about my health. She didn't want me to do any of these challenges, but she knows how my mind works. She knows once it is set it is hard to change.

She also realised what it meant to me and reluctantly agreed we might at least go to the pool and give it a go. Gently, she persuaded Kelly to let me try. Off we went quietly to the pool. We didn't spread the word and we kept it away from social media.

I slid into the water and started to swim but I didn't get far. I panicked. It was early and the pool was gloomy and dimly lit, with a low ceiling. Everything was very quiet and still. Only Lucy, Nicole and Kelly were there with me. I could feel the pressure climbing on top of me as I lowered myself into the water.

Very soon, I was falling a long way behind Lucy. She was stopping and looking over her shoulder for me. My breathing was all wrong and

I couldn't hit my rhythm. It was as if I'd been thrown back to the start of my training when I could barely swim a length. Nothing felt right. My chest was tightening. I stopped and Lucy stopped and came back to talk to me.

I was building myself into quite a state, thinking I had to get the swim done because I was falling behind schedule for the day. Kelly came to the poolside, knelt down and said, 'I'll give you one more chance.' I swam off and gave it one more go but the truth had dawned on me. I wasn't able to do this.

Physically and mentally, I was so low. I had crashed from feeling positive and focused to feeling as though I wanted to get out as soon as possible and get away from this dark and oppressive pool.

Karen arrived to find me slumped in the changing room like a broken man. I left her busy with jobs at the hotel that morning saying I felt great and wanted to do it. She had watched me breaking through barriers in the previous challenges and she always believed in me. Not today. To be withdrawn for a second time was a massive setback. I felt totally crushed. I tried to bounce back and I couldn't do it. It was harder to swallow than being withdrawn on the previous day.

I don't think I have ever been lower than in those moments when I thought the challenge might be over. It felt as though I had let the team and supporters down. I was worried the donations would dry up and that the charity would suffer.

Making it worse in my mind, Day Six was in Hampshire and most of the routes for the cycling and running were in and around Southampton. We were closer to home, people were coming out to see me and cheer me on and I was unable to take part.

It was a major disappointment even if it was the right thing to do. I climbed into one of the cars to offer some morale support and watched as the cyclists threw off the shackles. Professor Tim Underwood, a leading cancer surgeon and a keen cyclist, was there. So was Andre Couzens, a training mate and a friend of Andrew's.

Andre is a real powerhouse on the bike. They would have ridden at my speed had I been out there but I wasn't and this was like the Tour de France.

Andrew and Gary were feeling the change of pace because they had already covered close to 600 miles in the week. Tim and Andre came in fresh and went for it. They went from averaging around 15 mph when I was with them on the bike to an average of 19 mph across the two days without me.

It was great to see them going strong but I reached a point where I just wanted to get out of there and check in at the hotel. I was finding the day increasingly stressful and was beginning to feel unwell. There was still a big question mark about my participation on Day Seven, which was heightening my anxiety because I was desperate to reach the £1 millon target and I knew we were so close.

I started to burn up with a temperature. I was shaking and feeling nauseous. It felt like a flu coming on. One minute I was red hot and the next freezing cold. I started throwing up. It quickly became a truly horrendous day.

In the hotel room, I sat on the toilet clinging to Karen with my arms around her waist and my head on her chest. Luke was with us, becoming very concerned, and poor Kenzie was on her second day of filming in Manchester for the BBC, worried sick having to be away from us.

Outrageous as it sounds, we withheld all of this from Kelly. I was so desperate to complete the last day and I was sure I would feel better in the morning. I didn't want her to see me in this state and rule me out, because I looked and felt more ill than I had at any point on any of these three ultra-endurance challenges.

We thought it was important that, given the efforts the team were going to, one of us should join in with them, even it was just to stop them worrying about me as much. Karen went out to join the final couple of miles of the run. Luke stayed with me in the room with his fiancée, Connie.

I was so bad that they refused to leave my bedside, in case I had another turn. News spread that we were staying in the hotel and a large crowd gathered at the finishing point. We could hear the cheers as the runners arrived.

Despite all these people that had come to see me, and all the people running for the team, I could not get out of bed to thank them. I couldn't even make it across the room to the window and give them a wave. I wanted to go downstairs and clap them all in. I wanted to say thank you but I could not face standing up. Luke and Connie looked out from the window and described the scene. I just wanted to close my eyes and go to sleep.

When Kelly came in with pizzas in the evening, I was conscious of the need to eat if I was to have any chance of taking part on the final day. My inability to take on enough calories had been the single biggest problem on this challenge.

I forced down a couple of slices and started to feel slightly better. My optimism flickered. Maybe I was picking up. Maybe I was through the worst of it. I had no idea how I would feel in the morning, and only the previous day I had been in hospital, but the food seemed to provide a mini kick-start.

* * *

I woke the next morning feeling like a different person. There were no signs of illness and my body felt well rested. Physically, I knew I had it in me from the moment I opened my eyes. I was feeling positive. I spoke to Kelly and assured her I could do this. She checked me over and was happy for me to give it a go under her close observation.

To have a green light from Kelly, from a medical point of view, was great. Then, I knew I was going to make that finish line, even if I had to crawl over it. There would be other mental barriers to overcome but I knew I was back in Southampton and in familiar surroundings. The weather was nice, clear blue skies. I was in a good place and I knew the lay of the land. To start the day, I was swimming in a light and airy pool where I had done a lot of my training with Lucy.

There was a wobble almost as soon as I was in the water, a flashback to the day before and doubt wriggled into my mind. Briefly, it threw me. I lost my rhythm again and could feel the panic tighten across my chest but this time I composed myself, relaxed into the swim and enjoyed it.

The rest of the swim went without incident. It was great to be back and once I completed that 2.4 miles in the pool, I knew I was going to make it through the day. I punched the air and celebrated with Lucy at the end. The rest of the team were gathered poolside, all clapping and cheering. It was the first celebration.

* * *

We switched the order of the other two disciplines and did the run after the swim to enable us to take part in the Southampton Marathon, which was a mid-morning start. There was a buzz around the city created by the other runners and the crowds. I lined up at the start with someone dressed up as the cookie monster.

Quite a few of the support team ran the first half-marathon circuit with me. Luke, Liam Edgar and Matt Le Tissier were among them. Kelly, Deano and others joined me for sections of the second lap of 13 miles, as the race quietened down and the runners became a little more spaced out.

I do love to run and I was running in a city I knew so well. I had grown up on these streets and there were sections of the route where I had trained over the years. The course took me within a couple of hundred yards of my house. I wanted to savour it and remember it. One thing I have learned from the challenges is that the highs are all too fleeting and it is important to embrace and enjoy them.

As I crossed the Itchen Bridge, there was a clear view of the whole city. I could see the docks and the sea, as well as St Mary's Stadium and Albion Towers where it had all started for me, and there was a golden glow to the moment.

There were times like this at different stages of different challenges. Maybe not as many as I would have liked but, here, after two difficult days, I felt fit and physically strong and knew I was going to reach the finish. I felt revived. There was a pain in my knee but adrenalin was pumping around my body, and Kelly was instructing me to slow down and remember there was a 112-mile bike ride still to come.

It was a powerful feeling to be in such a good place, positive in my mind and at ease with what had happened over the previous couple of days. When I look back at the photographs and video footage from the Iron Fran challenge, I can see in my face how different that last day was. There were traces of the sheer fatigue and tiredness that came with this level of extreme physical activity, but the smile is genuine. I could not have said the same on previous days.

It had been the same during the Big Run and the Big Race: the last day was always something else, incomparable to the rest. The disappointment of being medically withdrawn on Day Five and Day Six of Iron Fran quickly faded and being out there, competing on Day Seven was the most important part of that. If I had not been allowed to attempt Day Seven, for whatever reason, I don't think it would have felt the same. I am so very pleased I could do that day.

There were heart-to-heart conversations during the days when I was withdrawn. My family asked how I would reflect on the challenge knowing I would not be completing seven in seven. They knew what I was like and that I might look back and feel it was incomplete.

But, as I ran the Southampton Marathon, I knew there would be no lingering disappointment. For one thing, it was the right decision to be withdrawn. The other, I had nothing more to give. The choices made were the right ones and I had no regrets.

These were the closing stages after months of training. I knew all the work that had gone into this challenge, but I don't mean by me. I mean by my family, who made all manner of sacrifices. I put them under enormous pressure when I decided to embark on these projects, both with the amount of time they required and the emotional strain I put everyone under as they watched me struggle.

None of this would have been possible without Karen, Luke and Kenzie: Team Benali. They are my world. They are my drive and my purpose. They have been beside me every minute and every step of this journey, sharing the ecstasy and the torture. We have the most incredible family bond and I count my lucky stars every single day that they are mine.

Another vital element was the unswerving support of a wider group of individuals who came together as Team Benali developed from the four of us to become a much bigger collective. To the support crew, family, friends and those at Cancer Research UK who all believed in me and shared a passion to raise as much money as possible to help and improve people's lives – and of course to all those who made donations – thank you from the bottom of my heart. The combined effort and spirit was clear for everyone to see on the Iron Fran challenge.

When I could not go on, my fantastic team refused to stop. I should have known they would step up to the plate. None of them signed up for this outcome. Nobody trained or prepared for the physical ordeal in the way I did, and yet the team members – not to mention complete strangers who came together and joined in – fought through the different elements of the triathlon and made sure our challenge continued.

Then all the love and messages of support that poured in gave me strength when I was in pain and finding it tough. All of these things made me determined not to quit and to finish what I had started.

Personally, I made it through five Iron Man triathlons in seven days. As a team, we completed the full seven and the donations actually gathered pace as I began to suffer.

The text-to-donate figures monitored daily by Tom and Shelley from Cancer Research UK more than doubled on Day Four, closing in on £10,000 a day, stayed at this sort of level for two days and then went up again on Day Seven to more than £12,000. There were other ways to donate online, and these figures increased significantly from Day Four onwards as well. National media interest was soaring and the story of my personal struggle was spreading across social media, and the profile of the Iron Fran challenge went up. We were closing in on the million-pound mark as I completed Day Seven.

I was a patron for the Dave Wellman Cancer Trust before I started out on the first challenge. I had a reasonable idea about the brilliant work they do at Cancer Research UK without fully understanding what really goes on. I learned much more during the course of our three challenges, and it reinforces the key role played by fundraising. Over the last 40 years, the 10-year cancer survival rate has doubled from 25 per cent to 50 per cent. It is down to the research funded and carried out by charities such as Cancer Research UK. Hopefully one day they can help find a cure.

We lost dear friends and family throughout our journey and we met people we would never have met without this undertaking. We made lifelong friends. Families engaged in their own cancer struggles regularly came out to meet us. The team spent more time with them than I was able to. I was out on the road covering the miles but they would get to know them, and listen to their personal stories.

On the first day of the first challenge, the Big Run in August 2014, a young man who had cancer, and his family, came to see us off in Newcastle. They brought cakes for the team and asked if they could follow us along the route to Sunderland, which, of course, they were welcome to do. As we said our goodbyes, they told us they would try to be there in Southampton on the final day, three weeks later. Sadly, they did not make it. His illness took hold and he died soon afterwards. It was a privilege for us to meet all these people and to hear their stories of courage as the disease touched their lives. They lifted our hearts. They provided us with motivation and inspired us. They kept us going through the tough moments.

These were the thoughts driving me towards the finish line of the Southampton Marathon and it was wonderful to have so much support lining the streets, especially after some of the isolated, quiet stretches earlier in the week. Anyone who has run a marathon will know the feeling of elation when crossing the finish line is simply incomparable. To do so after the week I had been through – and knowing this was my last challenge at least for a while – felt better than ever.

* * *

Only the bike ride to go, and the organisers of the marathon allowed us to start it by heading back out along the finishing straight, in the opposite direction to the runners. What a great send-off. The crowds were still in place and they cheered us on our way. I knew this New Forest route well, it was one we used for training and there was a big group out with us. We had grown from just myself, Andrew and Gary riding on the first day, out of Manchester, to this enormous peloton on the final day with friends, staff and volunteers from Cancer Research UK, and others who just came along on their bikes and joined in. There were 30 or 40 bikes with me at one point.

With the help of a company called 418, we used social media, the tracker on the website and local radio updates to let everyone know where we would be riding. It must have worked well because the support along the roads was incredible. There were crowds of people standing outside pubs we rode past. There were banners and Saints flags.

It was like a carnival, and the atmosphere ramped up as we ticked the miles off. We rode past a wedding in the New Forest near Lyndhurst. They were having their photos taken when suddenly our crowd of cyclists came by. We all stopped and said congratulations.

As we turned back into the city for the finish, the busier it became. It was like a social ride, and everyone was having a ball and grinning ear to ear. Certainly, it was far removed from those bleak days spent struggling up hills in the middle of nowhere, deflated and shattered with the wind howling and the rain pouring down. The fatigue accumulated from swimming 2.4 miles in the morning and running 26.2 miles in a marathon was eclipsed by the sheer thrill of being on the home straight.

I had no idea what the finish line was going to look like. The team didn't divulge any details. It was a day I had tried to visualise during months of training. I knew the route back into the city like the back of my hand. We came out of the New Forest and headed through Southampton's suburbs to the finish line at the Civic Centre and we flew towards it.

I break out in goosebumps when I think of the final turn into Guildhall Square and seeing thousands of people there waiting for us. It was dark and the Guildhall was lit up in purple, the Cancer Research UK colours.

Pete Dixon had arranged for digital screens to be set up, flashing up images from the last seven days of the challenge. There was a DJ, and Kenzie was on the microphone after flying home from her filming in Manchester. We weren't sure she would be back in time but she got a lift from the airport to the finish line, and was there just in time to meet us.

There were media teams everywhere, and the all-important ice-cream van. Some of those Benali masks, which we placed on seats for Saints fans at St Mary's Stadium for the final lap of the Big Race, made a reappearance. I could see them dotted around the crowd.

It was an amazing party atmosphere. I knew we were close to our fundraising target and the team informed me we were not there officially, but we could be certain of hitting the magical £1 million once the text-donations from the day had been added to our running total.

Six years, 3,100 miles, countless hours of work from myself and the team, and we had done it. The week certainly had not panned out quite as I planned but the final day surpassed all expectations and left me with a true sense of pride and achievement.

There I was, at the top of the Guildhall steps feeling like I was on top of the world.

* * *

Never again, I thought as I woke without an alarm at 5 a.m., pulled back the curtains and stared at the Iron Fran motorhome dominating the driveway. Well, certainly nothing on the same scale. We reached our target and I found my limits. This time, I did not wake the next day with any urge to put myself through it all over again. At least, not any time soon.

It was a Monday morning and my body was in a mess after swimming for 12 miles, cycling for 560 miles and running for 131 miles over the course of the previous week, and I needed to give it time to recover.

I booked in for some sessions with a chiropractor and enjoyed the chance to catch up with my family before returning to my work as a media pundit and motivational speaker. They filled me in on all the stories from behind the scenes of Iron Fran and we went through the piles of laundry and set about returning stacks of hired equipment to the right places. I knew all sorts of things would have been unfolding without my knowledge during the hours when I was on the road.

One of the nicest parts of being back home was to see our black Labrador, Ben, again. He was 14 and no longer in the shape to join me on the challenge as he did for the first one. We were heartbroken five months later when we had to say goodbye to him. He was the most faithful, loyal and loving friend any man could wish for, as well as the perfect training partner.

Luke and I went to watch England playing cricket at the Ageas Bowl, in Southampton, and settled back into normal life again. The bike went back in the garage, and after the euphoric high of completing the challenge and reaching our fundraising target, we were back to wondering what we might have for tea.

We went along to the last game of the season at Southampton where Kenzie interviewed me at the side of the pitch and they presented me with a shirt. On the back, they printed 'Iron Fran' and '£1 million' and they made a presentation to me in the boardroom.

I have loved the club for as long as I can remember and it was hard when the relationship broke down. But it has come full circle. I was delighted when they offered me a role as an official ambassador for the club and the Saints Foundation, which does amazing work in the community.

All of this recognition has been overwhelming, but the biggest shock came six months after Iron Fran when I sat at my desk and opened a very formal-looking letter, which told me I was to be included in the New Year's Honours with an MBE for services to cancer patients. None of this was my intention at the outset. Unfortunately, due to Covid, we have not yet been to the palace to collect the award.

The Big Run, the Big Race and Iron Fran have changed me as a person. They pushed and tested my body and my character to its absolute limits. We have made many special memories as a group of people and we managed to do some good with the fundraising.

I hope others who shared the journey can feel uplifted by the experience, and I am humbled to think people can look at what we achieved, the challenges we took on and the problems we overcame, and think about pushing their own boundaries.

Occasionally, a letter drops through the door or an email lands in my inbox, from someone who says they were inspired by what we did to take on a challenge of their own and to do something they thought beyond them. It always makes me happy.

I was the wide-eyed schoolboy who could not walk past The Dell without stopping to take a closer look and dream about a life as a professional footballer, playing for Southampton. I went on to represent my hometown club on 389 occasions at the highest level of football. I have spent my entire life in Southampton and I feel privileged to have received the Freedom of the City.

I had a dream to raise a million pounds for charity. It wasn't easy. It took us five years, but we made it. With a positive mind-set, a spirit of determination and the right people around you, it is truly amazing what you can do. Anything is possible. I know that, now.

ACKNOWLEDGEMENTS

With thanks to all those I played with and against during my footballing days. Teammates and opponents. Those I kicked and who kicked me. Those who coached me. Those who inspired me and believed in me. Those who helped me to achieve my dream of playing the beautiful game and representing Southampton Football Club. It was everything I imagined it would be and more.

Thank you to Saints fans everywhere for making the club what it is, such a special family club, and for taking me to their hearts. I wish there had been more goals and fewer red cards but there are no regrets.

Through my three fundraising challenges, thank you to everyone involved from the humble beginnings of the Big Run to the major operation that was Iron Fran. There are too many to name but without them, none of it would have been possible. I will always be incredibly grateful to the efforts of my support team for the work they did and for the time and energy devoted. Those who kept me going when I wanted to stop. Those who picked me up and reminded me why we were doing it.

To all those who sponsored us and put their faith in us. To Cancer Research UK for their help and advice. Those who spread the word and, of course, everyone who came to run with us or to cheer us along and made donations to take us to our million pound target.

Thanks to Matt Barlow for agreeing to bring my story to life. To all at Bloomsbury, agents and editors who worked so hard to bring the project together. Those who agreed to share their memories of our time together and contribute.

Thank you, to you, for reading my story so far.

Thank you to my family and close friends for their unwavering and heartfelt support.

And finally to Team Benali, my whole world. Karrie, the love of my life and my soul mate, my son Luke, my best mate and stat man and my daughter Kenz, you will always be my little girl with a smile that can light up any room. You three complete me and have been with me every step of the way, you made me realise anything is possible.

INDEX